81019

December
1979

To the Opera Maniac
from his long suffering
wife

with love xxxxx.

# In My Own Key

# ELISABETH SÖDERSTRÖM

# *In My Own Key*

Translated from the Swedish
by Joan Tate

HAMISH HAMILTON
LONDON

First published in Great Britain 1979
by Hamish Hamilton Limited
Garden House,
57–59 Long Acre, London WC2E 9JZ

Copyright © 1978, 1979 by Elisabeth Söderström

This translation copyright © 1979 Hamish Hamilton Ltd
Originally published by Albert Bonniers Forlag, Stockholm 1978
as *I min tonart*

British Library Cataloguing in Publication Data
Söderström, Elisabeth
  In my own key.
  1. Söderström, Elisabeth
  2. Singers—Biography
  I. Title
  782.1'092'4      ML420.S/
  ISBN 0–241–10318–5

Printed in Great Britain by Bristol Typesetting Co Ltd,
Barton Manor, St Philips, Bristol

# Contents

# Illustrations

## Photo Credits

# 1 / In the Wings

Her poor mind is confused, her thoughts whirling. She has just bidden her lover farewell, a last farewell. Honour and morality forbid her to go with him. She is bound to a man she does not love and to a mother-in-law who torments them both. She cannot go on living.

Death . . . does it frighten her? No. She consoles herself with the thought that birds will fly over her grave. Flowers will grow there, pale blue, golden yellow, dark red and purple. How beautiful the world is . . . and yet: 'I must die.'

She gathers up her courage and hurls herself into the Volga . . . and falls on to a mattress lying on a small wagon which is swiftly wheeled out into the wings. '*Vite, Madame, levez-vous* . . . Quick, Madame, get up!' Swift hands tear off her shawl, pour a bucket of water over her head and place a soaking wet shawl round her shoulders. Strong arms lift her up and carry her 'lifeless' body on to the stage so that Tichon Kabanoff has a corpse to throw himself over as he sobs out: 'Katya! Katya!'

Is it wrong of me to describe what happens in the wings? An artist has to work through what can be seen from the auditorium. But sometimes you feel like describing your problems and trying to explain why in your everyday life, you cannot always behave like an 'ordinary' person.

A*                                                           I

Many people ask me why I am so often ironic about life in general and my profession in particular. It is quite simply that I have to be, to keep a balance between involvement in the most profound tragedies and the cruel awakening when stage practicalities claim your attention and make you forget the inspiration. Distance is essential, as simultaneously, you have to switch on the whole range of emotions.

When in *Katya Kabanova* I hurtle flat on my face into the wings, I laugh and joke with the stagehands about 'one single to the graveyard, please'. When forty-five seconds later I am lying 'dead' on the stage, I am back in the tragedy, not thinking it remotely foolish. I *am* dead and have stopped breathing.

It is often tempting to try to explain to outsiders that our work does not involve the glamorous life that many people imagine we live. Some years ago, for instance, I was rung up by one of our more aggressive newspapers and asked if I were not ashamed of being a high-income earner.

'What do you mean? Do you think I lie on a sofa eating chocolates and raking in the cheques? My profession is ruthless and much harder than you could possibly imagine. There's no question of security when you have to live off such a sensitive instrument as a voice. You have to study for years. You aren't just staking everything on yourself, either, but also on the patience and time of your family. You work round the clock at what is called memorising. And when it comes to the point, a miserable little cold or such an idiotic thing as a piece of bread getting stuck in your throat can ruin all your preliminary work and make it impossible to present the result of your labours.'

I spoke with warmth for half-an-hour at that interview, given over the telephone. What came out in the newspaper was: 'Elisabeth Söderström says: "My job is sweat, phlegm and dirty feet".'

2

That same evening, a weeping woman rang me up. 'Never again can I go to the opera,' she said. 'Never again will I enjoy the beauty of it all. I'll just be thinking about their horrible sweaty bodies, spit and dirty feet.'

She rang several days in a row, this unhappy woman, and the whole family tried to console her. We asked her to try to forget this shock and instead feel as artists themselves do when they are on stage. While you are living through the drama and music, such banal disturbances as, for instance, the secretions of the body, simply don't exist. If you concentrated on outward circumstances, how could you ever persuade yourself or others that you were a fifteen-year-old Japanese girl, or a seventeen-year-old youth in love? And how would you dare sing straight into the face of your fellow-singer . . . that's not really possible without a few drops of saliva. . .

When the performance is over, you find that even on those nights when you have been a hundred per cent absorbed in your rôle, somewhere in your mind you have also registered how things have gone.

I am like a mine when I return to the dressing-room or the artists' room . . . the slightest jolt and I explode.

For several hours after the curtain falls I go through in my mind every single note and gesture in my performance, grieving over those that have not succeeded. The few moments on stage when *everything* gells are desperately short, and the others soon take over. Perhaps you have to react in this way to be constantly stimulated to try again, to seek even more closely what you are striving for.

The fact that you are dissatisfied should also be kept from those who have been in the audience and have experienced the performance in quite a different way.

My mother was once sitting beside me in the dressing-room after an opera performance. While I was taking my make-up off, a number of visitors came in, wonderfully friendly and enthusiastic people who wanted to thank me.

'You were fantastic!'

'No, I wasn't,' I said. "*That* didn't work, and *that* wasn't good and *that* was almost painfully bad . . .'

Then the next person came in, and without being warned by the previous person's bewildered expression, he said: 'Beautiful! You sang like an angel!'

'How can you say that, when my voice wouldn't obey me and I had to breathe in the middle of a phrase and the top note in the aria was just off and wasn't alive, and . . . and . . .'

Then my mother whispered in my ear: 'Don't keep telling them how bad you are.'

Although you don't believe people who praise you and you are hurt if someone makes a critical judgement, you are also enormously dependent on hearing comments after a night when you have revealed your whole inner self in public. When the applause is over and the 'minor rôles' and dressers have gone home, the thunderous silence that descends in the dressing-room corridor brings with it an emptiness which even if you need it to get back to reality, also conjures up all your doubts.

The moment of truth. You are no longer the person you have been hiding yourself inside for so long. Now you have to go home to your real life . . .

# 2 / What Makes a Good Opera Singer?

After a concert I gave at the university in Frostburg, Maryland, in the United States, I was requested the next morning to answer questions put by the students.

I had greeted them cheerfully, and for a moment there was a solemn silence. Then the first question came: 'Why did you become an opera-singer?'

The way the question had been put was rather disconcerting, so I asked in return: 'Were you at my concert yesterday, and if so, do you think I ought to change profession?'

When we had sorted out what the young man had really meant and that he thought I seemed too normal to be occupied with anything so exotic and alien as opera, I took the opportunity to talk about how opera can be so very much more than what it appeared to be to anyone who had never set foot inside an opera house. I was also able to tell them that not all opera singers were like Maria Callas, the singer who, to the majority of Americans, personifies the profession.

I also told them that in my case, the profession had probably chosen me instead of the other way round. I had wanted to be an actress, but as I had sung all my life, I took the chance when I was invited to appear in an opera, and then I stayed on the opera stage.

I was born with a singing voice. I learnt from my nurse the entire repertoire of the Salvation Army. Together, we sang such songs as:

> *In a ward in a children's hospital,*
> *Where the little white beds stand.*

When I was only two or three years old, this treasure trove of songs came in useful.

My parents often gave large parties and, quite naturally, they wanted their small daughter to come in to meet their guests. The daughter, however, dressed in white organdie with pale blue bows in her hair, flatly refused, often in storms of tears, to be dragged in to meet them. But one day, my father had an idea and asked me to go in and sing something.

So it became a tradition at home that when all the guests had arrived, the Shy Daughter was brought in to sing, for instance, *Jesus loves all little children*, before they all went in to dinner, for their food and drink.

Later, when I was older, to my mother's accompaniment I used to sing a more varied repertoire, among others many of the tenor arias I had heard my father sing, such as Cavaradossi's Song to life from *Tosca* or Johnson's impassioned outburst in Act III of *The Girl of the Golden West* by Puccini, in which he pleas that Minnie shall think he has gone free. It must have sounded rather touching, coming from a ten-year-old little girl, but as far as I remember, the guests did not laugh.

Often when thinking back, smiling a little, too, at these rather foolish appearances, I realise how grateful I am to my parents' friends for allowing me to think they were taking me seriously. That early training for appearing in public was enormously useful. You learnt to recognise the thumping of your heart and the dryness of your mouth that occur

6

as you wait for the first chords, and gradually, you discover how to breathe so that you have enough oxygen to sing without coughing, despite all the cigar and cigarette smoke.

During my schooldays in Stockholm, we were constantly giving soirées and theatrical performances. During the war years, there was always some charitable cause working on behalf of refugees and other needy people, and the Nya Elementar School for Girls was one of the most active in helping refugees. We had a small stage in the assembly hall and in Shakespearean fashion, we transformed that into all kinds of environments. Learning to appear on a stage in this practical way was invaluable. It is almost impossible to explain in theory what it feels like to be confronted with the energy of an assembled audience. Thoughts and concentration of minds generate a force you can almost touch. During the very first few seconds on the stage, you can feel how the rest of the evening is going to go. The quality of the audience, if I may put it that way, is felt immediately.

I should say that what is most important when you choose a profession such as mine must be that you long to be on the stage. Madame Skilondz, my beloved singing-teacher, said: 'To be an opera-singer you need spirit, and spirit, and spirit . . . and it does no harm if you have a bit of voice, too.' In my case, she was preaching to a terribly shy adolescent who at the start of her singing studies needed help most of all in gaining self-reliance.

Singing lessons can be terribly testing to your patience, for both teacher and student. Training a voice to bear the strains it will have to take on the opera stage is often monotonous and tedious work. The student immediately wants to throw herself into the great arias and cannot understand why her teacher says instead: 'Go home now and keep quiet until your next lesson.' Singing scales and exercises instead

7

of Butterfly's aria is torture, when you are dreaming of living out your adolescent problems in music.

One of Sweden's greatest singers, Christina Nilsson (1843-1921) is said to have remarked that to be able to stand the physical strain of being an opera-singer, you had to be 'as strong as a sailor, no, as a cart-horse.' Although we are not exposed today to the enormous differences in temperature artists used to have to endure when the stage was lit by gas and the air in the wings was icy, there are still sufficient situations in which good physical condition is a great help.

Christina Nilsson married a Spanish count and became Countess Casa de Miranda. She was celebrated all over the world and became very rich. On one of her few return visits to Sweden, a reporter asked her: 'Isn't it difficult to remain humble when one is borne on the hands of both high and low?' 'No,' came the answer. 'Definitely not. I know that it may take only the slightest breeze and . . .', here she pointed to her throat, 'everything is over.'

In an article headed *Advice to Young Singers*, Christina Nilsson stressed how important it was to exercise your body and to eat the right kind of food to keep fit for the demands of an operatic career. She knew that lengthy rôles were a great strain and that you had to maintain the effort until the curtain went down on the last act. It meant never being out of breath, not even during rapid movements on stage while you were singing. Producers of today love testing breathing techniques of artists in this way.

It is very interesting to observe how good breathing technique can help a person not only physically, but also mentally. I can confirm that there is a great deal in the expression 'singing and songs breed noble feelings'! Sometimes I have even been able to sing away a headache or a cold. They say

8

it is something to do with the oxygen supply and the circulation of the blood in your body. Diaphragm breathing and good teaching of singing should be on every school curriculum.

Sometimes during my years of schooling, I tried telephoning Madame Skilondz to be excused a lesson. 'I've got such a terrible cold, I can't come today.'

I nearly always got the same answer: 'That's the moment to come. You have to learn how to sing when you're not feeling well. Anyone can sing when well. In our profession, you have to know how to sing when you're indisposed. During my career, out of a hundred evenings, I was quite well only about five times. Come now.'

I grumbled and groused, but I am grateful to her today. Out of hundreds of evenings, I think I have been quite free of troubles at the most twice. And when I started, there was no such thing as being off sick. You lived on being able to work, and if you couldn't work, you had nothing to live on. It was as simple as that.

Many young people want to be artists in order to live out their emotions on the stage, to let themselves go. What a lovely expression. I suppose I also thought that at the start, and I certainly took every opportunity. As opera repertoire is full of emotional explosions, there were plenty of chances. But it was a dreadful disappointment to find that only a very small fraction of an uninhibited performance ever reaches the audience. Indeed, the audience usually finds it boring or painful. To influence an audience emotionally, you have to control the performance.

One of my first great tragic rôles was that of Regina, the girl in Hindemith's *Mathis der Maler*, an opera that contains a great deal of human suffering. I wept most of the evening. At that time, in 1950, there was no mascara that withstood

9

water, so the result was that the mascara dissolved, your eyes gummed up, your nose began to run and your voice became strangled. Nothing I had wanted to convey to the audience reached them. The stinging mascara was good for me . . . I learnt to weep less 'for real', and then the effect on the stage was much better.

In my next rôle, the same thing happened. *Der rote Stiefel* by Heinrich Sutermeister contained a scene in which I had to stand downstage expressing mute despair for fifty-six beats, while my beloved danced himself to death. The tears poured down and so did the mascara. Birgit Cullberg, the choreographer of the production, noticed my dilemma and gave me a pot of a new kind of mascara that did not dissolve in water. That opened up a whole range of new possibilities in the silent scenes, but was it any better? I doubt it.

I went on weeping as Tatyana in *Eugen Onegin*, a rôle from which it took me almost five years to dry out. I identified myself so completely with every moment of Pushkin's adolescent girl that I simply couldn't stop weeping away all the best scenes, in that way spoiling them musically. For in opera, the music goes on all the time and you have no time at all to swallow down floods of tears. Swallow . . . and your next note comes a beat too late.

When after many years of bitter learning, you at last realise that you can adapt your emotions to the rhythm of the music, then the creation of a scene takes on a new dimension. At long last, I realised what my teacher at the opera school had meant when he had said : 'It is not you, Miss Söderström, who is to feel. It is the audience. It is not a matter of inspiration. It is a matter of suggestion.'

Though I would prefer to put it this way : empathy plus controlled expression of feelings, as well as the ability to wind down after a performance, all go to creating a professional artist who has something to offer in the world of music without perishing in the process.

One also has to have a professional name, a short, preferably two-syllabled name . . . and if both names start with the same letter, so much the better.

When in 1955 I made my first operatic guest appearance in Salzburg, a number of international impresarios paid me a great deal of attention and requested private conversations with me.

At lunches and dinners, I was offered a brilliant future if that particular agent was allowed to launch me. But . . . there was always a 'but'.

One said: 'You must stop being so frightfully natural. People don't want natural opera-singers.'

The second said: 'You must change your name. You can't go by the name of Söderström if you want to have an international career.'

The third said: 'Are you married? For God's sake, don't let anyone hear that. You can't possibly make a career for yourself if they know you're married.'

So I swallowed, curtseyed and said: 'Thank you very much, but I don't want a career. I just want to sing a little and I want to live with my husband in Sweden. And I want to keep my maiden name, because I've already been using that for quite a long time.'

Then things ran their course, and my engagements took me out into the great wide world, despite the fact that I did not obey those impresarios.

In the States, my 'naturalness' was an advantage. I was often displayed like a rare animal in a circus. 'Come and meet Miss Söderström. She's so natural. Listen to her, isn't she cute?'

At the Met, they added the two dots over the o's in my name. This was because if you tried to turn ö into oe, as they had done with Jussi Björling, then my name became too long to go in one row on the posters.

They spell my name with ö in England now, too, but I remember a small incident before that started. After a première at Glyndebourne one night, I went to a small hotel where we were to celebrate with the artists. In the lobby was a telephone kiosk and one of the critics was telephoning through his review of the evening's performance. 'No, no, no! S-O-E-D-E-R-S-T-R-O-E-M! Yes, I know it sounds idiotic, but that's how she spells it!' Then I realised it would have been much easier for a great many people if I had changed my name. Anna Olow, which in fact is also my name, would have been a fantastic professional name, but why should everything be easy?

Whether one should be married or not . . . that I think really depends on whether you have managed to find someone who can think of putting up with sharing his or her life with an artist and all that that entails.

To be an opera-singer involves isolating yourself quite considerably. Having to memorise long rôles means that you are often very silent and boring company. Many artists also have to keep quiet during the day before major performances to spare their voices. Some of my colleagues do not say a single word on such days, and if they have to communicate something, they whisper.

If one is to survive such a life as ours, one must learn one very important thing . . . to be able to be alone with yourself. Whether you are nervous, happy or unhappy, there will be many moments in your life when you cannot share your feelings with anyone else, when you are alone with no one else but yourself and your sensitive little instrument, and you wait the endlessly long hours before at last it is time to go to the place where your audience is assembled. Then it is a question of being able to live with yourself and knowing how to occupy yourself to keep your mental balance.

Good nerves and mental balance . . . yes, they are often necessary as you go through the mill as a singer. The mere fact that everything you do will be judged publicly, in itself takes some getting used to, learning that all those malicious remarks perhaps are not so malicious as they seem the day after the première, that praise is often apportioned with consideration to other artists on their way up or down. I remember from my earliest years that what hurt most was receiving the enormous jubilation of an audience at the theatre in the evening, being overwhelmed with flowers and compliments, and then the following morning receiving the cold showers of icy comments in the press. But one does get used to it by putting oneself into a larger context and then everything falls into proportion.

One of the things I find difficult to get used to, however, is that as a 'famous' person, one is expected to have the ability to produce, at the drop of a hat, clever and amusing and – first and foremost – readable comments on almost anything in question-and-answer form. Had I known that when I started taking singing lessons, I think I would definitely have tried to go to evening classes in journalism at the same time.

One day, for instance, my telephone rang just as I was on my way out. 'Just a question and answer, that's all. It won't take long.'

'I can't. I have a taxi waiting outside. I'm on my way to Arlanda airport.'

'Just one quick question . . .'

'Well?'

'Have we any right to be happy?'

There . . . just try delivering in one minute a brief and comprehensive reply to that, a reply which can be read and interpreted and twisted and turned and criticised and despised, and, who knows, which might even influence the mind of another person.

# 3/ How Can You Learn All That by Heart?

I never cease to marvel over the human brain, its capacity and function, nor do I cease to be irritated that I cannot force my brain to do something. Patience and persistent training . . . and then all you can do is to hope that at the moment you need it, the knowledge that has been fed into your brain will be delivered promptly in a fraction of a second. 'How can you learn all that by heart?' is a question that is as common as 'What do you do all day?' Exactly. That *is* what we do all day. Drumming into our heads and memorising text and music. People have either a visual memory or an aural memory, or more usually a combination of both.

If I have to learn a score, I first read the text. Then I tackle the music and the text together, and I usually find it is the music that stays in my mind first. If I come to a place in the music which is difficult musically, I try to 'photograph' the notes in my mind, and that works surprisingly often. I can stand on a stage or a platform and 'read' by heart . . . by which I mean I see the notes in front of me on my inner vision, so that it seems as if I have the score in front of me.

But that does not always work, and if while I have been learning it, I have had different scores or arrangements, then I'm sunk. Then learning functions only mechanically. I remember once when I was doing a difficult but enormously emotional piece that made the audience ecstatic. It contained a number of technically very difficult passages and the only way I could cope was by counting one-two-three-four, one-two-three, one-two-three-four-five, six etc. I happened to reveal this trick to someone who had been very moved by the concert, thus depriving that person of the illusion of the profound empathy of art. But . . at the same time, I was deep in the text and experienced it just as powerfully as the person in the audience. Another part of me was working on technicalities.

Whichever technique you use for learning, there are very few short cuts. The safest way is to go through your lines over and over again and drill them into your mind. In my case, a memorising process occurs which starts the moment I tackle a rôle or a song, and I am not free of it until what I have to learn is firmly fixed in my mind. Then I can read a page of a book again and grasp what is there. While I'm learning something, I can read the same page of a book fifty times and not really register its contents, because my brain is occupied with other words.

In a society so concerned with regulated working hours and 'man hours'—that bureaucratic linguistic flower—and holidays and so on, I do sometimes find myself extremely alienated, not to say maladjusted. I can't stop working just because I have left the theatre at the end of the day's rehearsals. My mind does not stop memorising and the working hours taken to create an interpretation of a rôle are usually as many as the hours of the day and night.

The same applies to preparations for artistic performances, which really do not look like work, but which are absolutely necessary to achieve the best possible result. If a work-controller were to come to my home in the afternoon before a major performance, he would find me curled up under the bedclothes. 'I'm working,' I would tell him, because that is part of my work. Warmth and rest are essential for my instrument to function. But how could I put such work into tidy statistical tables?

The hours after a performance are also part of my work. No one who has undertaken an intensive interpretation of a rôle can relax immediately after the performance. It takes many hours before you calm down. Are those also counted as working hours?

Fixed working hours have become very important today. When I started in this profession, we rehearsed until every possibility had been explored that day. I find it very difficult to adjust to the new system of definite times and breaks. If, for instance, you are rehearsing a new rôle and go down to the theatre for stage rehearsals at, shall we say, half-past ten in the morning, then you are hardly likely to get into the right mood and atmosphere for an intense love-scene or a death-scene for about half-an-hour. Then just as things are warming up and you begin to have some idea what the scene means emotionally, just as some give-and-take starts between the artists . . . then it's time for a break. Whether you want to or not, you have to take a legal break. In some ways this reminds me of that old saying: 'First he raped me, then we had coffee, and then he raped me again.'

There could be a risk of rehearsals of the violently emotional utterances that occur in most operas being regarded in the same foolish light: 'Strangle Desdemona, break for coffee and then commit suicide. Please begin . . . and you should be dead by half-past three.'

Because of cuts in working hours, it is becoming more and more difficult to go through a whole rôle in *one* rehearsal. Only the dress rehearsal allows us to play the whole opera through its full length . . . which can be considerable, when it comes to opera. Then something may happen as befell me in *Madame Butterfly*. At the last rehearsal before the first night, we had got as far as the moment when Butterfly sings her heartrending farewell to the child and is about to take up the knife to commit hara-kiri. As an artist, one has staked everything in the way of emotions and the moment of release comes as she thrusts the knife into her body and is thus liberated herself. But no, that moment occurred at one minute past three, so there wasn't time for it. Everyone says thank you very much and departs, leaving behind an unreleased artist with all the pain a Japanese woman has stored up and saved for the decisive blow. What do you do?

Well, you have a family, so you go out and buy food for dinner and you see in every butcher's knife the knife that should put an end to the suffering you carry within your heart.

Shorter working hours within an opera house also mean that you have to do the studying for a part more mechanically, almost like factory work instead of a craft. Personally, I find this unsatisfactory, as unsatisfactory as travelling round with a rôle and then with no rehearsals, just stepping into a finished production. It works . . . but the result can never be a consummate artistic event.

Apropos being a travelling artist, that also brings with it other problems, if you belong to a Swedish opera company as well. When you make a guest appearance abroad, you nearly always sing the opera in its original language, while in Sweden, operas are usually performed in Swedish, a practice which I have always advocated.

But your brain does not always keep up. In this respect, I can refer to my appearance as Octavian in *Der Rosen-kavalier*. I originally sang the rôle abroad and in German, the first time in an incredibly well-rehearsed production that was performed fifteen times in succession. So my lines had been thoroughly learnt and stood in my mind as firmly as a rock.

Then I went back to Sweden, and soon afterwards received an invitation to sing the part in Stockholm, in Swedish. I learnt the Swedish translation, and although we did not have all that many rehearsals, I thought I knew the text.

But when it came to the performance, I was nervous and the result was I forgot what I had most recently learnt. But the German text was there and as I sang, I translated directly from German into Swedish. Naturally, not all the words fitted in with the score properly. Sometimes notes were left over and sometimes I had far too many syllables for a phrase. I tried to gather my wits and stared in despair at the prompter, who in her turn stared back at me as if I had fallen from the moon. At first she had no idea what I was up to.

After the performance, we went through what had happened and laughed about it, but the next time, she knew how to help me.

When I start on a new opera rôle, I first read through the text in the original language, then I sing through the music. If I am to sing the opera in Swedish, I can then check that the translation phrases the music in the same way as in the original. Unfortunately this is all too often not the case. Many translators take the trouble to make the text sound well in Swedish and even tolerable to read in print, happily sacrificing a note or two here and there.

What usually happens in such a translation is that a word that is important to the action is in incorrect time if you compare it with the original text. We often work with foreign producers who do not understand Swedish, and they are very surprised when you carry out an action in the 'wrong' place, that is, not on the beat where it occurs in the original. As the music is composed from the original text, I think it is unforgivable to ignore such things when an opera is being translated, and today, I always insist on rewriting the text when I find it is not possible to interpret the music as the composer had intended.

When you are being trained as an opera-singer, it is important to learn the languages in which you are going to be singing. That saves a lot of trouble and a great deal of work. Naturally, if you find it easy to imitate, and most singers do, the part can be learnt parrot-fashion, but the interpretation will almost certainly be better if you know exactly what you are saying!

I remember a television broadcast in London, in which I was to sing the end of the last act of *Bohème* together with an English tenor. We were singing in Italian, a language he did not know. During the rehearsals, when we came to the lovely introductory phrase to the final duet '*O soave fanciulla* . . . Oh, beautiful maiden', he turned to the great window in the décor and made a great sweeping gesture towards the full moon outside.

I interrupted and said: 'Um, sorry, but I am over here!' He nodded and smiled and we started again, and he repeated his gesture, so I interrupted him again. We started sorting the situation out, and then it appeared that he had always sung the part in English before and the phrase had then always been 'How bright is the moonlight!' One could not blame him, because that is what he thought '*O soave fanciulla*' meant.

Translators often like changing small words unnecessarily, too. In the last act of *Bohème*, Mimi says in one place: '*Tu non mi lasci?*' to which Rodolfo replies: '*No, no!*' This means literally 'You're not leaving me? No, no.' That is also in one of the translations we have used at the Opera House in Stockholm. Then along comes a new translator who is shamed into thinking that we cannot have anything so simple, and he changes it to 'I beg you to stay'. To which, of course, Rodolfo should reply : 'Yes, yes.'

But then it can happen that two artists meet and sing from different translations, and it has actually happened that Mimi said 'I beg you to stay' and then received the original's 'No, no' in reply. Painful.

When stage rehearsals of an opera rôle start, musical studies should be complete, and you should know your part by heart. When actors memorise their parts, they often walk about with their scripts, trying out their lines and memorising the text by placing their different remarks in different places on the stage. 'When I'm standing by the chair, then I must say this or that'. In opera rôles, the music has already largely determined what you are to think and feel, so at stage rehearsals it is a question of polishing nuances. Singing an opera rôle is technically so difficult that you have to get the work out of the way by placing the music in your body before you can begin to think about placing your body on the stage.

When I think myself into a personality, I often start by imagining how that person walks. It sometimes helps to wear the shoes you are going to wear with your costume, even in the early stages of the work. You move differently in high or low-heeled shoes, boots or slippers. Walking immediately gives you the key to the character.

If you are acting in a crinoline, it is almost essential to wear the frame that holds the dress during rehearsals. All distances and movements become so dependent on your clothes. It has happened that I have rehearsed an elegant faint on the stage floor, quite against the etiquette of 1700, only to discover that that etiquette existed for quite practical reasons. When you did the same scene in a crinoline and all the rest, the inevitable happened and the whole costume ballooned several feet above the person who had fainted.

As work on the rôle continues, there is more and more you have to know. What did the world look like in the days we are acting in? How did these people spend the rest of their time, outside the brief moments we are allowed to meet them? What did they read? What did they talk about? Sometimes I walk round imagining the smells surrounding them. Especially in the eighteenth century, there must have been strong smells of dirt and perfume.

The more you become involved in what is called the life of luxury a countess or a marschallin lived in the eighteenth century, the more sorry you feel for those women, imprisoned in etiquette, a surface morality and idleness, and at the same time envied! No wonder they so often had migraines.

It was wonderful to tackle a rôle such as Christine Storch in *Intermezzo* by Richard Strauss. This woman is a portrait of his wife, who is portrayed by her contemporaries in general and by Alma Mahler in particular as an unusually unpleasant, insolent and hysterical woman, quite without understanding for her husband. I have often reacted against the insinuating Viennese stories about her, and when I studied how lovingly Strauss portrayed her in this opera, I could understand her problems very much better. She was one of those women who had had to give up her own profession as an opera-singer, and instead become the head of a household in which all the important things were carried out by people who knew their jobs. Her husband was constantly away, and on the few occasions when he was at home, he sat at her side in silence, sunk in his composing. I remember after one of the performances, a lady came into my dressing-room. She was the wife of a famous singer, and in tears, she said to me: 'Thank you for showing what it is like for me, and for making us who have no profession of our own seem sympathetic.'

The more deeply I involve myself in a part, the more my thoughts revolve round understanding what that character is thinking about between lines. That is most difficult in stage productions. While you are standing listening to what the other people are singing, you think the thoughts the character would have thought, not your own. All too often, you see artists on the opera stage turning 'private' between their lines, and this is a favourite subject for those who parody opera, making singers clear their throats, or spit, or get themselves into another 'singing position', while they wait for their next lines.

When you act the same part over and over again and want to maintain controlled thinking, you have to learn a certain technique. It doesn't always work.

I have often sung in Britten's opera *The Turn of the Screw*, in Sweden called *A Curious Story*. It is about a young governess whose first appointment is in a strange place. She agrees to look after two orphan children, whose previous governess has died. In the house is an old housekeeper, and it is she who reveals to the governess that the man she thinks she has seen in the garden and outside the library window, is a servant who one night fell and broke his neck. When the governess next goes into the schoolroom, her predecessor is sitting there at the desk.

The children appear to have contact with these dead people . . . or have they? Is it all the imagination of a highly-strung young woman, who is being tested in this her first attempt to educate children and who is jealous of her predecessor? And thus misinterprets events and what she hears?

The first time I played this part under Göran Gentele's direction, we performed on the Blanche Theatre annexe stage for twenty-six consecutive nights. It was a terribly intense production. Production, décor and music in perfect unity created a nerveracking atmosphere. The stage and auditorium were both small and intimate, and to expose yourself as Göran demanded, you had to be inside the skin of the character you were supposed to be for every single moment. Every evening, I had to go through the tortured thoughts that were tormenting the governess' mind. After about ten performances, I noticed that I had begun to think differently, unconsciously interpreting her way of registering what was happening around her.

Now, afterwards, I often wonder to what extent this influenced my interpretation of the rôle, how much was noticed outwardly, and whether it made the audience think in a different way about the real circumstances in the story. I suppose I shall never know.

Operas have stories and also prompters who can help you when your memory fails you. Memorising songs that describe nature in poetic terms is really difficult. I have ground my teeth many a time over *Winde* that *sausen* or *rauschen* or *brausen*. It is all the same to me, but it is painful, for you can find yourself on the wrong line of the music if you happen to choose the wrong verb. In my work, there is a great deal of learning to do, and to cope with it all, I have to keep my brain in trim. I have noticed that you can train your brain in the same way as you train up your muscles. I need to keep my brain going between learning parts, too, so I do crosswords and cryptograms, and I read a great deal. The more I learn at any one time, the faster it

1 Susanna in *Le Nozze di Figaro* (Metropolitan Opera House, New York)

*Der Rosenkavalier*

2 (a) Octavian (Glyndebourne, 1959)

2 (b) The Marschallin
(Geneva, 1973)

3 (a) Adina in *L'Elisir d'Amore* (Metropolitan, New York)

3 (b) The Governess in *The Turn of the Screw* (Royal Opera House, Stockholm)

4 (a) Ighino in Pfitzner's *Palestrina* (Salzburg)

4 (b) Tatiana in *Eugène One*
(Glyndebourne, 1968)

5 to 8　The Countess in *Capriccio* at Glyndebourne
(a) In the 1963 production

(b) With Günther
Rennert

(c) In the 1973 production

(d) With Kerstin Meyer as Clairon

goes. What I learn too quickly vanishes the moment I have given the performances.

A good way of being certain of your homework is to do it six months before you are to perform the work. Then you let it rest, and when you take it up again, text and music have in some way sunk deeper into the tracks in your mind, and you don't feel nervous about dropping words or notes in performance, as you do if you have studied a part quickly.

'Don't you ever go quite blank?'' is another question I am often asked. Yes, this does happen, and for various reasons. Lack of concentration is probably the most common one. It can also happen that the learning period has been too short.

Once I was to sing Britten's *Les Illuminations* for the first time, in the Royal Festival Hall in London, I had studied it in Stockholm, learnt it on my own, and so had not had anyone to hear me. The language is rather convoluted French and the music is quite difficult to memorise. However, the rehearsal with the orchestra went well, I remembered everything and it was gratifying music to sing. The final rehearsal also went well without any hitches.

I went to my hotel, had a good meal and lay down to sleep. I felt calm when I woke up and dressed, and did my make-up and hair in a good mood. In the taxi on the way to the concert hall, I began to feel uneasy. When I got to the artists' room, I was nervous and unsure of my memory. As the minutes ticked by, I built up a kind of hysteria that convinced me that my voice would not carry, my memory would not function and the best thing would be to cancel the performance. I was on my way to the conductor's room to inform him of my decision when they came to fetch me for my entrance. Beads of sweat were running down my temples, my lovely piled-up hair-do slowly collapsed like an unsuccessful soufflé and I explained that there was no point in my going out on to the platform, as I wouldn't be able to sing anyhow!

The concert was being broadcast direct on the radio, the announcer had finished his introduction and the green lamp was on. The conductor, one of my greatest friends and one of the conductors with whom I most preferred to sing, stared at me as if I had been transformed into Mrs Hyde. He had no idea what was going on. The sympathetic attendant, who had probably seen a great many nervous artists in the place where I was standing, solved the problem for me by taking hold of one arm. The conductor grasped the other, and mumbling calming words such as 'It'll be all right. It'll be fine,' they dragged me to the door and literally shoved me up the steps to the platform. As if in a dream, I heard the roar of waves . . . or was it applause . . . and I staggered like a robot between the musicians.

At the place where I was to stand was a chair they had placed there that morning for me to sit on during the rehearsal. They had forgotten to take it away for the evening, and it saved me. In my strange state, I failed to see it and walked straight into it. The chair fell over, I fell over and the audience laughed and applauded such unexpected entertainment.

When people are hysterical, I have heard that you are supposed to give them a slap. This was like a slap for me and I woke up! I still had a lump of ice where my heart was supposed to be, and although I thought I would never remember the first line of the text, I also felt some confidence returning; let them play the introduction and then something will probably come. I smiled at the conductor and settled myself into place. The orchestra launched into the introduction of the first song and when it was time for me to come in, I was standing there like two people, the one contentedly listening, while the other sang something that the first person recognised, vaguely . . .

It was not the best concert I have given in my life, and a critic pointed out that I had sung a sharp instead of a flat in one of the songs, but there was no scandal. Afterwards, I wondered what had caused such a nightmare. Perhaps I had worked too intensively during the week and was more tired than I was aware of. Perhaps it was unconscious terror of performing Britten's music to an audience and critics who knew it better than I did.

# 4/ *First Steps in Opera*

Signe Hebbe is the name of a Swedish opera-singer of the 1800s known for her statuesque posture and her marvellous movements on the stage. It was said that she resembled a Greek statue and carried herself like a queen.

She taught many people, and among the most famous of her pupils were Anders de Wahl and Ragnar Hyltén-Cavallius. The latter became in his turn a teacher at the Opera School. I was fortunate enough to be taught by him . . . just how fortunate, I did not discover for some years. When I was accepted into the Opera School, I had a great complex about my body. I had been told I was too tall in relation to my voice. A lyrical singer should preferably be no taller than 155-160 centimetres. I was 169. I tried to hide those nine centimetres by hunching up and sometimes bending my knees, foolishly enough. My hands were too big and I nearly always wore shoes that were too tight to try to make my feet look smaller.

But then we were given the following schooling . . . learn to use your bodies. Learn to deal with your hands and feet. You have to know how to make large gestures. Learn them first, make them often, and then you can abandon them if they are not necessary. Learn how to move in a crinoline and in Greek garments. Work hard at ballet and movements, and do them in front of a mirror.

We went to the school with all our modern ideas. Acting should be natural on the stage. We were against the old 'grand-opera' style, which we thought artificial. Cavallius snorted: 'Natural, huh! You have to know the craft first, then you can start being natural.' How right he was.

When jokes are made about the 'grand-opera style' of acting, it is seldom considered that in the old days it was not possible to convey anything with facial expressions, because it was too dark on the stage. If you were to embody an emotional expression, you have to use gestures of which everyone knew the meaning. Gradually, stage-lighting got better and gestures could be modified to a more natural form, but opera is still often performed on enormous stages, with an orchestra pit several metres wide separating you from the audience. Even today, large movements are often necessary for the audience to sense that one is 'acting'. All too often people are heard complaining that opera-singers just stand there singing.

I think it is a great pity that there is not more teaching of 'body language' all over the world. When I see a performance by a singer with a fantastic voice, but who cannot differentiate between a positive and negative gesture, I feel very ill-at-ease. If you don't know what you mean by a gesture, then that gesture should definitely not be used.

Another thing that makes me feel quite ill is when an artist standing facing the audience and about to move to the left starts off with the right foot. That was lesson number one at the Opera School. If you are to move to the left, make sure you have your weight on your right foot and start with the left.

When I think of the thousands of hours artists spend

polishing their voices, it seems to me almost criminal to let them appear in opera without knowing how to use body-language on stage.

I often hear people from the audience defending such artists by saying: 'Oh, I just shut my eyes and listen and enjoy it.' No, opera shouldn't be like that!

When Cavallius was directing, if you tried to act little reactions in your rôle, you would hear such remarks as: 'Miss Söderström, do you want to go to the lavatory?' 'No, Sir.' 'Well, then, for God's sake stand still. The audience loves to see you standing still.'

Cavallius 'acted' as he directed, making every single movement he wanted from his students and then demanding to see them repeated. When I made my début as 'Martha' during my Opera School years, I rebelled several times and refused to carry out scenes as he prescribed. The result was that he went to the Director of the Opera and complained that it was impossible to work with me. 'Miss Söderström is so brutal!' Harald André took it all quite calmly and managed to mediate, so it all ended happily. We compromised and in time we became the best of friends, and as I said before, as the years went by, I became more and more grateful to my teacher and understood more and more of what he had wished to teach me.

The Director of the Opera, Harald André, was one of our country's pathfinders in quite a different way from Cavallius. His great interest was in the external details of production. For instance, he brought the cyclorama to the Swedish opera stage, and he used a lighting technique he had learnt in Germany and which had not been seen before in Sweden. A malicious story about him says that during a rehearsal with lights, he called to the stage manager: 'Switch on the working lights so that I can see what the singers are doing!'

30

I played Pamina in a production of *The Magic Flute* he directed, and as I was used to every gesture being prescribed by the director, I asked him on one occasion: 'Tell me, sir, what does Pamina do to show her anxiety when Tamino does not answer her questions?' André smiled his nice warm smile and said: 'Try rocking the top half of your body a little, Miss Söderström.' That was his personal direction, and strangely enough it worked rather well. In this performance, he wished to create a mysterious atmosphere and had the whole of the Isis temple enveloped in thick mist. In this mist, we were to sing the trio in which Pamina takes farewell of Tamino before he is sent out on his trials.

The mist was so thick that we coughed more than we sang, so we complained to the director. 'Oh, if it troubles you, then I have to tell you it is ammonium chloride we're burning, the stuff the throat specialists use to cure sore throats. It's very good for you.' And so the mists remained.

When I complained to my singing-teacher, she just smiled benignly and said I should be glad I hadn't had to sing the Queen of the Night in André's first production of *The Magic Flute*. She had done so, and in one of her arias she had to make an entrance from the flies, lowered on a wire fastened to a steel frame on which she hardly had room to place her feet. To add to that, it so happened that on several nights she lost her foothold and sang the whole of this very demanding aria swinging in the leather harness fastened to the wire. It worked all right. What's a bit of smoke . . . huh . . .

André was past-master at large imposing productions. Like Cavallius, he loved having huge numbers of people on the stage. This meant that all young singers were always used in minor rôles or crowd scenes.

We were slaves in *Aida*, and pages in *Tannhäuser*, whose only task was to rush on crying 'Hallelujah' two minutes before the curtain came down in the last act. We were on stage almost every evening, and on nights when we weren't, we sat on lighting towers in the wings where we couldn't be seen from the stage and soaked up the achievements of our senior colleagues. A wonderful time.

It was presumed that we could take on minor rôles at short notice. The first time that happened to me at the Opera School was when Mr Sylvander, the embodiment of stage-manager, planning director, personnel-manager and welfare officer, rang me one Saturday morning and said: 'Miss Söderström, you're to come down to the theatre and fetch a part. You're to replace Brita Appelgren this evening.'

'But, Mr Sylvander, I can't dance.'

With horror, I saw myself trying to dance in place of the best ballerina in the theatre.

'I'm not a fool, Miss Söderström. This is a speaking part in *The Tales of Hoffmann*. You are to play Hoffmann's muse.'

I went down and fetched the part. It consisted of eight lines that were to be recited, while the orchestra played reminiscences of the phrases Hoffmann had sung earlier with Giulietta. The first lines were:

> But I, Hoffmann? The friend who so often
> In sorrowing moments sent thee comfort

With thumping heart and anxiety in my soul, I worked at the lines all day long at home in my room, and when evening came, I went down to the theatre, where Mr Sandberg, conductor of the Royal Opera House orchestra, played through the scene with me and checked that I knew my lines. Oh, yes, I knew them all right. Then.

I was helped with my make-up and into the grey chiffon veils that constituted my costume, and the time came. They took me on to the stage and put me inside a little cupboard.

'We wheel his cupboard on to the stage when Hoffmann starts dreaming, and when you hear the music, Miss Söderström, start reciting.'

It was extraordinary the way my heart thumped. Suddenly, it grew quite dark. 'Now!' hissed Sylvander, and the cupboard was wheeled on to the stage with me holding on to the sides so that I should not fall over. Then 'fiat lux,' a sea of light all round me! The sides of the cupboard were equipped with lights and the effect when these were all switched on was utterly overwhelming. I could neither see anything nor hear a note of the music. As it was the first time I had ever appeared on the stage during a performance, I did not know that sometimes when the orchestra played *pianissimo* in the pit, you could not hear a note up there. I waited and waited to hear the notes that would tell me to speak, but all I heard was an irritable voice, the prompter's, repeating. 'But I, Hoffmann . . . but, I Hoffmann!'

So in the end I said: 'But I, Hoffmann . . .' and then the cupboard was wheeled off. I need hardly say I wept all that night. I was also extremely surprised when at the end of the month I had to sign for fifteen kronor for my rôle in *Hoffmann*!

# 5/ Mozart

Mozart is altogether remarkable . . .

Such apparently simple and uncomplicated music that contains such worlds of emotions and atmosphere.

Most musicians I have met regard Mozart's music as the greatest, and it is to that world of beauty and purity they turn when they have exhausted all other sounds.

That apparent simplicity . . . is that the reason why the world is so full of Mozart experts, why there are so endlessly many ways of interpreting Mozart's music?

I remember one occasion when I was taking part in a festival week in Bern. I was to sing two Mozart rôles, the Countess in *The Marriage of Figaro* and Fiordiligi in *Cosi fan tutte*. The operas were being conducted by two different people, each one with quite a different interpretation of how Mozart should be performed.

As it was a festival, the artists came from all corners of the earth, and there was no time for long rehearsals. Our work on *Figaro* began by all of us sitting down with the conductor to listen to a brief explanation of the programme.

'Mozart's music is the purest in the world. Everything he has to say is in the music and not a note needs adding, so I do not wish you to sing any *appoggiaturas* or add any *cadenzas*. I will give you the tempo myself. Just take it naturally with no unnecessary *ritardandi*.'

So we performed *The Marriage of Figaro* with all the artists keeping their eyes glued on to the conductor, trying to remember to remove all grace-notes in the recitative . . .

The next day, we had a rehearsal with the conductor of *Cosi fan tutte*. 'Mozart was a brilliant emotional person. So we must interpret his music with all the involvement we can muster. It is very important that we differentiate in the recitatives between joyful and sorrowful tones of voice . . . that is, we shall do positive and energetic statements *without appoggiaturas* and plaintive ones *with*. I think we must have a *cadenza* in the *Per pieta* aria, and as artists nowadays are not used to improvising as they did in Mozart's time, I have written one out for you, Miss Söderström . . . here you are!'

So we sang a performance that in the hands of this man turned out to be very varied and lively, but once again we had to keep all our attention on what he was accentuating with his gestures in front of the orchestra. '*Ja, ja* . . .'

When I had sung the rôle of Susanna in *The Marriage of Figaro* for several years, one day I went to a rehearsal with an orchestral society. I had put the Rose aria that Susanna sings in the last act on to my programme. The conductor turned to me and asked in a friendly way: 'What tempo do you want for this aria?'

I cleared my throat: 'Well, what do you think would be suitable?'

'No, no, you must decide. I'll accompany you.'

I thought for a moment and then realised that during the last few years, I had probably sung Susanna under seven different conductors, each one of whom had his own idea of the character of the aria and thus also a different tempo. Obedient and well brought-up as I was by my Swedish musical education, I had simply followed. If it went too slowly for the breathing technique you had or didn't have, you tried to divide up the phrases as discreetly as possible. If it went too fast, you had to keep up as best you could and play the scenes more swiftly, at the same time hiding the fact that you were feeling harassed.

'No, I don't think I really know what tempo I want. Though, of course, perhaps we could go through the aria "by feel"? You see, this is actually the first time I have been allowed an opinion.'

An artist should be an instrument and fit in with the great orchestra, which consists of both musicians and artists. An artist should melt into the whole. But . . . an artist should also have his or her own personality and be able to produce his or her own personal interpretation of a rôle. Otherwise the artist is no artist; at least, not one of quality.

With regards to Susanna, I once sang the rôle under a conductor who was extremely sensitive. After the recitative before Susanna's Rose aria, there are two chords before the beginning of the actual introduction of the aria. On these two chords, I had to do two things . . . one, get up from the bench on which I was sitting, and two, pick a rose from the bush beside me. Pom . . . up. Pom . . . pick the rose.

Night after night, the same thing happened. After my last word in the recitative, I began the movement to get up . . . no pom. I was stuck in a kind of half-sitting posture until a chord at last sounded. Then I stretched out my hand . . . no pom . . . touched the rose . . . still no pom. One night, I even had time to smell the artificial rose for quite a long time before the 'pick-chord' came.

I went to see the conductor. 'It's like this, Maestro. I have a little problem with my scenes, and I wonder whether we could come to some agreement on the tempo for those two chords. I have to get up and pick a rose and it seems easier to do that directly, or I must at least know roughly when the chord is coming.'

'Yes, yes, I know . . . it's just that . . .' The conductor smiled nervously. 'I do so want those chords to come as a whisper, and I'm so frightened . . . as soon as I raise my hand only a tiny fraction to give a sign, I know it's going to be too loud . . . so I daren't lift my hand. And they won't play until I've given them a sign.' I swallowed my respect for conductors and asked whether he could possibly consider another solution. Couldn't the orchestra itself be allowed to fill in those two chords?

Lines of doubt and hurt distorted the face of the Maestro, but he was really a wonderfully fine musician and a warm personality. He was not offended, and instead we agreed that the next night he would make the suggestion to the orchestra. 'I won't conduct those two last chords. But may the devil take you if you don't play them pianissimo!'

'How thou my soul reneweth' pom-up, pom-rose. It worked . . . dolcissimo, pianissimo!

And the result? Well, at the next performance the Maestro overcame his terror and I was saved.

I usually quite cynically divide Mozart conductors into three categories: the slow, the fast, and those I prefer to sing with.

The latter category consists of conductors who succeed in finding the organic tempo for the music, by which I mean when I don't find it difficult and don't have to sneak a look at the conductor to see which tempo he has chosen for the transition from one movement to the next, or at the beginning or the end of an aria, or at a *rallentando* within an aria. Everything suddenly feels so natural. To be able to make music with such a person can in modern terms be described as akin to perfect sexual harmony.

The slowest *Figaro* I have ever sung was when I sang the Countess at a recording session with Klemperer, who at that great age probably interpreted the music differently from the way he had earlier on in his life. In one way, it was extremely interesting, because you suddenly heard details in the orchestral playing that you normally never distinguished in more ordinary interpretations. But it made great demands on your technique and your breath had to last out much longer. You also had to fill the phrases with more spiritual content, so to speak.

When this recording came out, I received a delightful letter, which I have kept. This is what it said : 'I have never before heard the Countess' arias sung at such a slow tempo. But I think it is wonderful, because in that way I can hear you for so much longer at a time.' That really is a compliment.

From that recording, I remember a moment when we were in the control-room, listening to a play-back. Reri Grist had sung the duet with Gabriel Bacquier, the duet in which the Count tries to seduce Susanna into a meeting in the park. Neither *lento* nor *adagio* is sufficient to describe the tempo, nor *largo*. Reri turned to Klemperer with her most delightful smile, but with despair behind it, and said : 'Oh, please, Herr Doktor, would it not be possible to take it at a slightly faster tempo. I find it so difficult to make love so slowly.'

A slightly lecherous spark lit up in Klemperer's eyes and he replied : 'What are you asking of me . . . I'm eighty-four . . .'

I have sung Mozart all over the world, but for me the extremes have been striking and unforgettable. There was one performance in Maple Leaf Garden in Toronto. The arena there is usually used for boxing-matches or six-day cycle races, and it seats fifteen thousand people. We played *Figaro* there during a tour with the Metropolitan Opera, and I think the picture of us the audience could see from their seats could not have been bigger than on an ordinary television screen at home. The sound was magnified with loudspeakers, so no doubt also sounded rather as if it were coming from a television set, or at best a broadcast—in stereo, perhaps.

The other 'extreme' occurred one cold Saturday night in the People's Park in Kramfors in Sweden. I remember someone asking one of the attendants walking round the park what time it started.

'We usually start throwing them out at about ten,' was he reply.

That was his job, of course, and he probably couldn't believe that the artists themselves did not know when *their* job started.

We were very cold that night, but we had a marvellously kind and patient audience sitting there wrapped up in rugs, as the auditorium had a roof but no walls. The applause sounded slightly muted, as it does when you clap your hands with gloves on, but an audience can make other sounds to show that a performance is being well received.

When we were finally gathered at the front of the stage for the end of the last act and seven throats were singing away as loudly as they were able, a curtain of mist formed by our combined breaths rose between us and the audience. And then with some terror, we noticed a cloud of midges in the beam of the spotlights, lured to this border-country between the bright stage and dark auditorium. You have to draw very deep breaths when you are singing such an ensemble and we did so without flinching. It was a record for me that evening . . . seven midges swallowed!

When we came to the end of the ensemble, it was probably just about ten o'clock. And true enough, that was when it started. A fairly well-oiled gentleman from the audience bellowed out from his seat : 'C'mon Mozart!'

He was thrown out. Pity!

# 6/ Some Producers

All through my earlier years on the opera stage, I was used to producers being mostly people who told me where I should go, where I should stand and which gestures I should make. My meeting with Günther Rennert showed me that production could be quite different.

The opera in which we were to work together was Pfitzner's *Palestrina*, a long, ponderous and profoundly psychological story. A formal, almost religious atmosphere pervaded the whole production, and this dampened my spirits. Rennert held long intellectual discussions in depth about every single detail in the music and text, twisting and turning every word to try out how they should be interpreted. All this in German . . . but I managed to keep up! I respected, admired and worshipped him, but that summer my tears flowed as profusely as the rain did over Salzburg.

The next time I worked with Rennert was at Glyndebourne. We were to perform *Elegy for Young Lovers*. W. H. Auden and Chester Kallman had jointly written a libretto that had been set to music by Hans Werner Henze.

There was a heat-wave on in England, the sun blazing down on the idyllic Sussex countryside, and the rehearsal rooms were unbearably stuffy even early in the morning. There was also already oppressive heat in the atmosphere between

Rennert and the two authors, who were sitting in on rehearsals. Auden's visionary way of describing these people did not impress the coldly intellectual Rennert.

I was playing the young woman-friend of a genius, who was loved by his contemporary, that is, his sixty-year-old secretary. I, in the play called Elizabeth, naturally fall in love with someone else, the twenty-three-year-old godson of the genius.

At the beginning of the opera, something that had occurred forty years previously is related. A young couple on their honeymoon, called Mack, come to a village in the Alps and then go on an outing that ends tragically. The young bridegroom falls down a ravine and is buried beneath the snow. Hilda Mack remains in the village and sits constantly by the window, awaiting his return. She thinks she hears her husband's voice telling her what will happen in the future. Hilda Mack has found refuge in the house of the 'genius' and he uses her visions in his writings.

In time, Mack's body is found. It has been frozen into the ice in a glacier, and the old woman again sees the beloved of her youth just as he has always looked in her inner vision.

One morning, we were to start rehearsing the scene in which Hilda Mack in a thrilling coloratura describes one of her visions. Dorothy Dorow was Hilda Mack and Kerstin Meyer was playing the secretary. Rennert came into the rehearsal room where we were all standing ready. He snapped 'good-morning', adding yet one more wrinkle to Auden's face, described at Glyndebourne as 'like an unmade bed.' Then he said to us: 'We shall do scene three today. I consider this scene unperformable. Please begin.' Then he sat down with his arms crossed while the *répétiteur* tentatively began to play the introductory music.

It was very bewildering to receive no instructions at all.

We placed ourselves rather haphazardly round the chair on which Dorothy was sitting. She began her song and Kerstin and I stood listening with roughly the expression Hofmannsthal in his instructions for *Der Rosenkavalier* gives to the Marschallin: *Mit einem undenfinierbarem Ausdruck.* (With an indefinable expression). Perhaps we were vaguely thinking about all the Bergman films we had seen. We stared straight at the audience, and I concentrated on imagining the bridegroom deep-frozen in the ice. That cooled one off a little in the heat, anyhow.

It worked. When the long scene was over and the singing and music had stopped, we heard a snorting laugh. It was the producer, who came towards us with his arms outstretched. '*Kinder, mit diesem Schwedischen Blick kann man ja alles machen!*' (My children, with that Swedish look one can achieve anything). And Ingmar Bergman has in fact demonstrated that, too . . .

When the rehearsals were transferred to the stage, Auden came into the auditorium one day after a good lunch, to watch. John Christie, the eccentric founder and owner of the Glyndebourne Opera house, was already there. He definitely did not enjoy the kind of opera that Henze-Auden had created, which was perhaps why he did not greet Auden, although Auden had already been there for several days. However, Auden plucked up courage and tapping Christie on the shoulder, he said: 'Mr Christie, I'm Auden.'

'Who?'

'Auden. I wrote this opera.'

'You shouldn't have,' said Christie.

My third part with Rennert was that of the Countess in Strauss' opera *Capriccio*, a difficult and demanding rôle. When I went to the first meeting with my producer this time, he came towards me until his intense eyes were about ten centimetres from mine. We stared at each other in silence for about a minute, and then Rennert said: '*Das Stück fällt mit der Gräffin*,' (This play stands or falls with the Countess) . . . and then we began to rehearse, I somewhat inhibited by the knowledge that it would be my fault if it turned out to be a fiasco.

When Götz Friedrich came to Stockholm to produce *Jenufa*, I felt it was just like going back to opera school where I had protested against Cavallius' way of forcing gestures on to me. I reacted strongly against his way of building up the performance in this way.

'I can't carry out definite movements until I know what sort of person I'm supposed to be, can I?' I said. 'I don't even know her yet.'

'But I do,' said Götz. 'Do it like this.'

Not until I saw the finished production, with the whole cast, décor, lights and orchestra, did I give way. I realised then that I was nothing but a small piece of a gigantic puzzle, and I was so impressed that I swallowed my objections to his interpretations of some of the scenes in the third act. Against my inner conviction, I played them as the producer wished me to. But it seemed cowardly and false, and I was very worried on the first night that the audience would unmask me.

I will never for one second forget the moment when the curtain went down on the last act at the première. It was deathly quiet in the auditorium for so long . . . then came an ovation that was quite deafening! My reaction was a hysterical flood of tears and I fell into Kerstin Meyer's arms with tears of relief pouring down my cheeks. As the curtain went up and down amid tumultuous applause, I tried to hide my face as best I could, and I remember Götz staring at me in astonishment. 'What's the matter with her?

Why's she crying? It went well.' '*Ja, ja . . .*'

Göran Gentele was a combination of these two types of producer, which was probably why it was so good to work with him. He demanded precision in scenes, so that you did exactly the same thing at every performance. But as we had built up each scene together quite logically, that was not difficult. There was only one way in which to play the scene.

Göran also had a sense of humour and used jargon that most of the company started adopting. After a rehearsal, he would come up on to the stage and say : 'Not bad. Not bad at all.' And we would all brighten. 'But was it good? No, like hell it wasn't. Now let's start again.'

Many of Göran Gentele's productions were thoroughly slated at their premières, but they remained in the repertoire for anything up to twenty years. It is quite interesting and moving to compare reviews of the first performance with those written about the same production when it appeared again a few years later and times were more suited to the style he represented.

The first time I was to sing Mélisande in Debussy's opera *Pelléas and Mélisande* was in a broadcast production in Swedish on the radio. This was conducted by a Frenchman, who afterwards insisted I should go to Monte Carlo and sing the same part in a French production.

So I learnt Mélisande's part in French and hoped I would have a good producer to help me with this difficult rôle. I arrived in Monte Carlo and went to the theatre to take part in the first musical rehearsal. The Opera House was in the Casino, so to get to your place of work, you had to pass the gambling rooms. But it was no hardship to abstain from gambling, as I was absolutely broke at the time and we were paid no advances.

The rest of the company were French, artists who had

sung their rôles for several years in this the national opera of France. No one seemed very keen on rehearsing, so when the conductor became enraged with the unfortunate pianist's failure in his attempts to play the difficult piano score, they all assisted by saying: 'Impossible, this is quite impossible.' It was decided to skip all piano rehearsals and instead wait for the arrival of the orchestra in three days' time. 'Au revoir.'

I turned cold with fright and modestly enquired whether I could meet the producer. A wall of chilly incomprehension grew up between me and the native French. 'What do you mean? Producer? We haven't got one. There's no need, as everyone knows this opera.' That night I cried myself to sleep at the hotel.

In the morning, I was a little more cheerful and decided to stay and try to carry out the assignment, despite everything. I went down to the shore with my piano score and to the calming sound of the waves beating against the rocks, I read the part over and over again, trying to put myself into the other parts as much as my own, trying to imagine how they would react in each situation.

When at last the time came for stage rehearsals, it turned out that the other artists had no desire whatsoever to waste their precious voices until they were paid. The only one to sing was me, and I did so in the places I guessed my phrases should come. As I received no cues whatsoever, they often came in the wrong places, and in the end both my courage and patience gave out. I threw myself into a rage of despair and told my fellow-artists in Swedish, French and English that they had damned well got to be so kind as to perform as they intended to.

My French colleagues looked at me as if they had just seen me for the first time. 'Have you got problems?' 'Yes, you might say so. I've never done this opera on the stage before!'

When they at last realised that there was *one* soprano in the whole world who had not sung Mélisande before, they were endlessly helpful. They led and pushed and shoved me round the stage, whispering in my ear every single reaction I ought to have. We became very good friends during this rehearsal, and that friendship continued right through the performances, which we managed to complete with reasonably good results.

There was one incident, however, that almost killed the tender feelings between Pelléas and his Mélisande. In the love scene when Mélisande is sitting high up in her tower window, while Pelléas sings his longing to her from the garden below, Debussy prescribed that at a certain moment, she is to let her long blonde hair down the wall. For Pelléas, the contact with her silky locks becomes an intensely sexual stimulus, inspiring a wonderful musical outburst. A deeply symbolic and very romantic scene.

My blonde hair consisted of a hideously ugly reddish-blonde plait, six feet long. I wound it round my arm and at the appropriate moment, I let it down far enough for Pelléas to catch it in his hands. At that very same instant, my lover leant backwards and looked up at me as he sang. The end of the plait landed straight in his mouth and his singing turned into a strangled gurgle. I jerked my head back in horror and the plait shot out of his mouth again. For the rest of the performance, Pelléas did not deign to give me another glance. He embraced me now and again with great passion, as the part demanded, but he could not bring himself to look at the person who had spoilt his very best phrase.

I still dream about it sometimes, and always wake up with beads of cold sweat on my forehead.

# 7 | Difficulties

In 1957, together with Erik Saedén, I made a recording of Swedish romantic songs. Peter Kempe, who was producing, asked me to sing some *Songes* by C. J. L. Almquist as they stand in *The Briar Rose Book (Törnrosens bok)*, that is, unaccompanied, and this turned out to be a lucky hit. Both the melodies and the texts were much more effective than if they had been produced with an accompaniment added later, and nowadays hardly anyone sings them except *a capella*.

In a radio interview on the theme of what is difficult, the interviewer asked me whether I found it difficult to stand quite alone on a stage and sing these songs, and I said then that there were both advantages and disadvantages. On the one hand, you feel slightly deserted and you miss the support an accompaniment has to offer, but on the other hand, you have greater freedom when it comes to deciding tempo and key.

I haven't absolute pitch, and when I sing unaccompanied *Songes* or folk-songs, I am probably never quite sure in which key I shall begin a song. But over the years, you acquire a kind of inbuilt feeling in the throat for where the notes lie, and usually it is never a problem to find the right pitch for a song that you often sing.

What I often find very difficult is to control the tension

and the fluttering of your heart that so easily arise before the start of a concert. For the first few minutes, I find it difficult to breathe calmly, and naturally that can be heard in the voice, as it does not flow freely from the throat and the notes become blurred and almost false until I manage to regain control of my means of expression. It is no use persuading yourself that you can do what you are about to do, or that the audience is friendly, or that you are on form, so you have no reason whatsoever to be nervous. I love standing on the stage. No one forces me to. I choose to do so quite voluntarily . . . and yet, every time I am to perform, I am gripped by this trembling for the first few minutes. Perhaps it is because I so fervently want it to go well. Perhaps you are nevertheless not sure whether the people sitting there listening are quite so friendly after all . . .

With the years and experience, I have acquired routines that help me over difficulties, and I have also learnt that an audience often seems to appreciate it if some little thing goes wrong. Once in the Queen Elizabeth Hall in London, I was going to introduce my concert of romantic songs, which was also being broadcast direct on the radio, with *Schlagende Herzen* (Beating hearts) by Strauss. To be quite sure that it would sound well right from the start, I went through the song with my accompanist in the artist's room. When we were on the platform a few minutes later, my brain reacted against singing the first verse again and went straight on to the second verse. This didn't match with the accompaniment and after a few moments' frantic searching to find the place, my accompanist, Martin Isepp, and I stared at each other, and so I said to the audience: 'Sorry, but I've slipped up. I'll have to start again from the beginning.' A great soughing went through the audience, and then turned into an icy silence as I started again on *Schlagende Herzen*.

Cold sweat cooled my flushed cheeks, but my voice rang freely and text and music came where they should. The audience's reaction was quite wonderful. They were just as relieved as I was, and the rest of the evening was a lovely experience, with them picking up every little nuance I achieved.

If I had not managed the song the second time, I think that would have meant cancelling the concert, as my nerves would probably never have coped with what my brain was up to.

I also often find it difficult not to be influenced by the music I hear around me, as, for instance, when I was taking part as soloist in Mahler's fourth symphony at the Vienna Festival. I sat on the platform for the first three movements, and those surroundings alone moved me. I could not help thinking about what an enormous amount of music had been played in this historic Musikverein, and how many fantastic artists had appeared there. Then the Vienna Philharmonic conducted by Claudio Abbado played the third movement, making all the dams inside me burst. I was so profoundly affected that I could not stop the tears running down my cheeks, and I had to try to hide them by bending my head right down.

Then the third movement came to an end, the fourth followed *attacca* and I had to stand up and sound like an angel from heaven *mit kindlich heiterem Ausdruck, durchaus ohne Parodie*, (with a happy, child-like expression, but without parody) it says in the score. I could hardly start by blowing my nose or clearing my throat. All I could do was to try to find a few notes, but unfortunately I probably sounded as if I had my mouth full of porridge.

One difficulty that the audience perhaps never thinks about often arises on the opera stage. When you are standing singing in very powerful passages, or if you have a colleague beside you singing *fortissimo*, you can hear nothing but the voice, not a note from the orchestra. If to cap it all you are as short-sighted as I am, the conductor's beat cannot tell you where you are in the music, either. Often when you are covering considerable distances on the stage, the orchestra can also become lost, and then you have to keep the beat of the music in your body, so that all the same you hear inside you what you should hear with your ears. One of the greatest tasks of the prompter is to help artists on stage fit their phrases into the right place in the flood of notes, even when they cannot hear that flood.

Operatic scores are naturally difficult to memorise because of their great range, as well as the fact that you have so many operas in your head at any one time, but on an opera stage, there are many ways of covering a gap in one's memory. You can hide behind the scenery or another character and get help from the prompter.

On the concert platform on the other hand, there are no such remedies, and you are very much more on your own. I often find it agonising to see a whole audience sitting there with the words in their hands, while I, poor creature, am standing before them in the painful situation that occasionally arises when one begins to think ahead. In the middle of a song, while you are automatically singing some phrase, your brain can go off on its own and start wondering what it says five lines lower down the page. This is a very peculiar phenomenon and painful for the victim. It has happened to me once or twice, when my eye has caught someone in the audience fixedly reading the programme while I am singing.

These moments when the brain functions on several planes simultaneously are probably very brief in reality, but they seem an eternity while you are standing there totally alone

51

and powerless to control what is happening. But it is typical of my profession that these brief moments etch themselves into your memory more than any other. All the things that have gone perfectly and excellently soon fade away, but the moments when you have slipped up or failed, you remember for ever. The same applies to reviews. You do not remember favourable comments nearly so well as criticism and harshly worded judgements. This in its turn adds to the fact that you can never take pride in any progress you may have made, and that you can never receive enough praise, appreciation or encouraging words on the way. God bless all those people who take the time and trouble to write a friendly word or two after some performance they have benefited from.

Another difficulty in this profession is to have inside you an understanding of how a rôle or song ought to be performed, and to know how much you are capable of when comments begin to reach you, particularly after a dress rehearsal. Then you are not only tired after a strenuous period of preparation, but also very vulnerable after this first meeting with an audience in that particular rôle. On such occasions, extra advice is often offered by everyone who considers there is a chance to influence you before the first night!

Naturally the reactions of people who have been in the auditorium should be listened to, but somewhere within oneself, one must sift and judge what can be of help in an interpretation one has worked on for so long. That *is* difficult.

In a recent production of *Rosenkavalier* in Stockholm, I was singing the part of the Marschallin. During the first act, my Octavian lost her voice completely. In the interval, the opera management tried desperately but unsuccessfully to find our second Octavian. 'We'll have to send the audience home . . .' they said. I was shocked at the thought, for I knew how people had been queuing for tickets, and I also knew that if one act had been played, people did not get their money back. 'You can't do that to my audience. Get me a costume. I'll sing the second act, and please keep trying to find another Octavian.'

It was only when I was standing in the wings, the silver rose in my hand, that it flashed through my mind: 'God, it must be eleven years since I sang this part . . .' Then I walked on to the stage, automatically singing and acting, and when there was something in the part I had forgotten, I just turned upstage or kept my mouth shut! My colleagues helped me enormously and the enthusiasm of the audience, who loved what was happening, created an electric atmosphere. I enjoyed myself tremendously and did not for one second find it difficult.

When I came off after the second act, I was told that Kerstin Meyer had come to help us, in spite of the fact that she had not sung Octavian for three years. So in the third act, I returned to the part of the Marschallin. When the curtain came down that evening, it sounded just like the crowd in a sports stadium.

The following morning, I thought to myself: 'Would I have agreed to sing the part of Octavian in that performance if it had been offered to me a week earlier?' Probably not. I would have found it too difficult after so many years.

# 8 / Can You See the Audience?

Once when I was very young, about nineteen or twenty, I gave a song recital at a school in Stockholm. A youth organisation ran evenings of folk-dancing, and in the intervals, there was usually some musical entertainment. I stood on the stage and looked out over the crowded hall full of young people of my own age; full, except the back row, where there were only two people, a boy and a girl locked together in an embrace.

I sang of love, tragic and fulfilled, of the countryside and children, successfully capturing everyone's interest . . . except those two in the back row. In my eagerness to capture their interest as well, I sang more and more intensely, but all in vain. They didn't once even glance at the stage. In the end, my patience snapped and I said: 'You two in the back row, you may think no one can see you, but I can, and if you don't stop kissing at once, I'm going.'

The audience's reaction was immediate. Everyone turned round and stared at the unfortunate lovers, who hastily sat up straight with a wide space between them. The concert went on with a very unhappy singer, who after the final song, rushed off into the wings and burst into floods of tears.

I have sometimes wondered why I could not stop myself doing what I did, and I have come to the conclusion that it was probably because for once I really could see the people in the audience. Usually individuals cannot be distinguished and people become an indefinite group that is felt rather than seen. You can hear them, but if they can be heard when you are singing, something is wrong. If you manage to capture the audience's interest, they hold their breath during the items and cough, sneeze and clear their throats in the pauses in between.

In most opera houses, the orchestra-pit is so large that a short-sighted person like myself cannot even see as far as the conductor, which can have its advantages. Also, the light directed straight at you is sufficiently strong that not even the people in the front row are distinguishable. What you do see if you stand near the edge of the stage are the lights in the orchestra-pit and also the musicians. As long as they are playing, they don't break your concentration, but sometimes you can fall right out of your rôle if you happen to see a member of the orchestra doing something he ought not to be doing.

But on smaller stages, I have been distracted by people in the audience. I remember, for instance, a performance of *Traviata*—I think it was in the beautiful old theatre in Borås in Sweden, where the orchestra-pit was no more than a few feet wide. I was kneeling in the last act, right down at the front of the stage, bidding farewell to life with the aria *Addio del passato*. Inspired by the rôle and the atmosphere that had built up during the evening, I was prepared to give my all of hunger for life and fear of death, when suddenly I was distracted by a winking light in the front row. The orchestra lights were being reflected in a glass. This glass was the lens of a pair of field-glasses. A man was sitting in the front row, hardly more than a few feet away from me, staring at me through binoculars. Naturally, I went on singing, the music relentlessly continuing and me simply following. But my concentration was shattered. I kept wondering: 'What can he see? What does he want to see? What do I look like?' It was not a good closing aria!

The most wonderful experience on the stage is when a whole audience holds its breath together with the artist. After a great outburst that rises to *fortissimo*, comes a pause, the length of which one decides oneself before continuing. Sensing that intense, hair-raising silence and holding the moment as long as it can stand, that is happiness!

Music is the only art-form that reaches the heart without having to pass through the brain, someone has said. From my own experience, I know that a voice can influence another person purely physically, the vibrations from it striking the nervous system like a touch. You are constantly reminded of the great responsibility you have as intermediary of emotionally laden music. Many people with unstable emotional lives find their way to the world of classical music, and for them you often become the embodiment of their experiences in the opera-house or concert-hall. When I began to perform, I had no idea my singing might intervene in the lives of other people and quite change them. It is a difficult balancing-feat to be able to remain professional when faced with people who through your art feel they have a personal relationship with you, and neither do you want to take away from them the experience in which they have been involved.

At a large concert arranged as the finale to the *Meet Modern Sweden* week in San Francisco, I sang to an audience of three thousand people. They were partly Swedes who lived in that part of the United States, but many other Americans had flocked in to hear Prince Bertil speak, to

9 In *Pelléas et Mélisande* at Covent Garden, with George Shirley, 1969

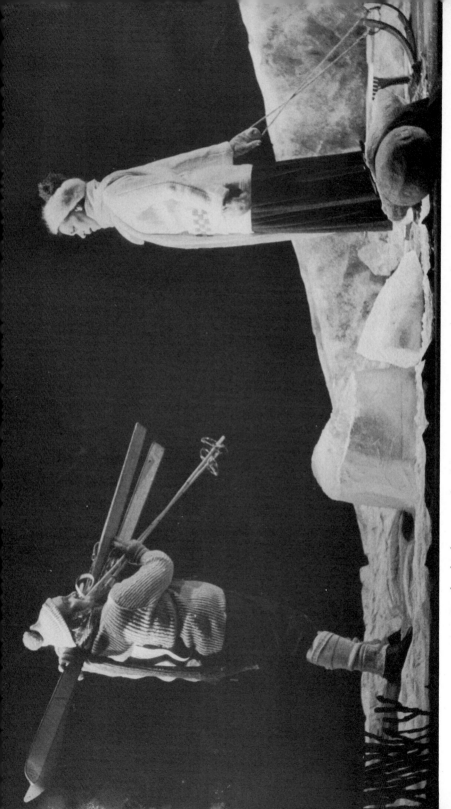

10 On the ski slopes at Glyndebourne in *Intermezzo*, 1974 with Alexander Oliver

11 (a) As Emilia Marty in *The Makropoulos Case*, Stockholm

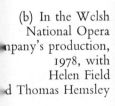

(b) In the Welsh National Opera npany's production, 1978, with Helen Field d Thomas Hemsley

12 As *Katya Kabanova* (San Francisco)

13 Rehearsing *Figaro* at
Covent Garden, 1967, with (*left
to right*) Tito Gobbi, Yvonne
Minton, Elizabeth Robson and
Geraint Evans

14 At Glyndebourne, 1961, with her sons Malcolm and Peter and the late
John Christie

15 As Leonora in *Fidelio* (Glyndebourne, 1979)

16 The author – a recent photograph

watch Swedish folk-dancing, hear the Swedish Glee Club singing, and join in on the concert I was giving. The presentation of my section was done in very grand style: 'And now ladies and gentlemen, we give you the Star of the Metropolitan Opera and Royal Opera of Stockholm . . . Miss Elisabeth Soederstroem!' Jubilation and a storm of applause. I made a deep curtsey and turned to give the pianist a sign that she could start. An agonised face appeared from behind the piano and my accompanist whispered frantically: 'There's no music rack on this piano,' and then she crept out.

Rather than have to make my entrance all over again, I stayed on the platform and smiled with some embarrassment at the audience, who were observing everything in watchful silence. The accompanist came back with a flushed face and signalled 'no luck' with an agonised expression. Then she beckoned to some committee members, at which they all vanished together.

I could not stand there in silence any longer, so I grasped the microphone and began explaining to the audience that a small problem had arisen and we had no music rack. While my friends were hunting one out, perhaps I could say a few words about the programme I had chosen.

I had time to say a few words not only about the programme, but also about Swedish singers and their international traditions, and Swedish cultural life in general and Jenny Lind in particular.

I even had time to tell the story about a brother and sister in the far north of Sweden who could not both afford to travel all that way to Stockholm to hear Caruso sing. So the brother went to the Opera, and on his return to the north, he sang to his sister so that she would know what Caruso had sounded like. Whereupon the sister said that she did not really care very much for Caruso's voice.

We had great fun, the audience and I, and the atmosphere was tiptop when the chairman of the festival committee finally announced that the piano had been delivered without a music rack. It had in fact been ordered for a concert by Rubinstein the night before and he never used music! The problem was solved by four gentlemen in white dinner-jackets standing round the piano holding the music up for the pianist. It was a touching sight, and I had to laugh every time I turned round to give a signal that we should start again. The audience laughed with me and the applause grew into ovation proportions.

After this exalted and relaxed concert, there was a reception at which the celebrities stood in a line and anyone could come and talk to them. I think nearly two thousand people wanted to shake hands with Prince Bertil.

I was standing in the line and was very moved to experience the heart-warming contact with people who had left Sweden so many years ago that their Swedish sounded archaic and old-fashioned. I pressed their hands and promised to give their love to 'old Sweden'.

When I eventually returned to Sweden, an item I couldn't really make out kept appearing in my harvest of letters. From all over the world, I kept receiving small romantic cards, often with printed verses and flowers and birds in pastel colours on them. Signed Frank Carson.

As there was never any sender's address on them, I put them in the heap marked 'unanswerable'. That heap contains a number of friendly letters in which I have been unable to decipher the signatures, so have not been able to write and thank the writers for their encouraging words. It also contains the nasty, malicious and bitter letters, not many, thank heavens, but always anonymous.

Over the years, there were many unanswered messages

from the mysterious Frank. Then one morning, the door-bell rang at home. It was nine o'clock in the morning. I opened the door. Outside stood a slight man in a light-coloured rain-coat. Dark hair and clear light-blue eyes. 'Here I am,' he said.

'Yes, I see, but . . . forgive me . . . who are you? Why . . . ?'

'I'm Frank. May I come in?'

Oh help! 'Yes, of course. Come in. Would you like some coffee . . . ?'

He came in. I gave him some coffee and I learnt all about Frank. He had been to my concert in San Francisco. He had felt the intense joy and enthusiasm in my music-making, and he had also felt that I was singing just for him. Hadn't I looked him straight in the eyes over and over again? This impression had been strengthened when he had introduced himself to me and I had pressed his hand *hard* and for a *long* time. From that moment on, he had but one thought in his head, to go to Sweden to confirm that what he had felt was true.

My heart turned icy cold as I heard him telling me how he had given up his work and hired himself out on various ships until gradually he had found one that was to take him to Stockholm. And now he was here.

Cowardly Elisabeth said she had a rehearsal at the Opera House, gave Frank a lift into town and dropped him off in the middle of Gustaf Adolf Square. I was quite prepared to find him standing outside my door again when I returned in the afternoon. But he did not come again. The cards from all over the world ceased falling into my letter-box. Four years went by before I again received a card from Frank. On it was written: 'I saw a movie with Marlene Dietrich. She was cruel to men but you are not. You told me to forget you, but I cannot.'

Had I had the slightest idea of such things when I started taking singing-lessons . . .

# 9/ Travels With a Voice

In all my childhood memories, journeys were always horrific experiences. I couldn't stand trains, boats or cars, and every time the family travelled, I knew this would involve feeling sick and shameful moments when I would 'behave badly' in public.

I simply cannot understand why I chose a life of constant travel. But when I was quite young, I developed a skilful technique of being sick with discretion, so when it came to flying and its paper-bags, I smiled in recognition. I often sang in Hamburg, and in the fifties, that short hop in relatively small planes between Copenhagen and Hamburg was an extremely unpleasant experience for me. The singer met by the representative of West German radio was usually pale-green and hardly conscious, and actually was more grateful when concert organisers did not send anyone to meet her.

Over the years, it has become easier and more comfortable to travel, and when I travel today, I am seldom sick. Instead I am afflicted with other miseries. A voice is a sensitive instrument and among the things it immediately reacts to is dry or damp air. On board a plane, the air is usually very dry and smoke-laden. In addition there is a constant draught from the many ventilators, and I only have to be on board for half an hour before my mucous membranes start protesting against such strains.

One of my male colleagues was once rung up from Munich early in the morning. Could he possibly throw himself on to a plane within an hour and come down and save that night's performance of *The Valkyrie*? Our heroic baritone rushed by taxi to Arlanda airport and just caught the plane. Once on board, he went straight to the lavatory, locked himself inside and stayed there until the plane landed at Munich. He knew that if he exposed his throat to the smoky air in the cabin, he would be incapable of singing when he got there. But this way meant that all was well for our hero.

It often seems to me that all travelling is arranged for men. Women have not the same strength to life heavy suitcases and trudge along endless corridors. Why didn't men realise that before they got rid of porters and short distances at airports? I think back with horror of the times I have travelled between Sweden and the USA with children of toddler age and with all the hand-luggage such a journey entails. After an Atlantic trip, the plane lands at six or seven o'clock in the morning, and at Kastrup in Copenhagen, one is met with miles and miles of corridor. You have to trudge on with three sleepy children, a carrier of books and toys, your fur coat over your arm, a bow-and-arrow too big to go into the suitcase, a machine-gun someone has kindly given the children for Christmas (this was before the days of terrorists) and of course you have bought the idiotic obligatory duty-free drink . . . a fiendish idea that adds to the traveller's burdens, no doubt thought up by men who don't consider a bottle of whisky a heavy burden?

I find the most tiring part of travelling is waiting in queues, at passport barriers, luggage-retrieval, buses and taxis. When my taxi finally stops outside the hotel entrance, I feel a great

61

sense of relief. I go up to the reception desk and smile exhaustedly. 'Welcome. Name please?' says the reception clerk, smiling back. When he hears Söderström, the smile usually fades. 'Oh, yes, a very quiet room for three nights . . .' and I can see his mind trying to work out whether this person is more sensitive to the noise of the lift, the restaurant or the garbage van? Perhaps she tolerates ordinary traffic?

Room number so and so, sleep well! Troublesome creature! Singers . . . we all know what they're like. May the devil take the lot of them.

The porter has over the years learnt that newly-arrived travellers have to be treated with caution and he chats about the weather. Then after a long walk through twisting corridors, you come to the door of the room that is to be your home for a few days. Then the inspection starts. Air-conditioning? Can I switch it off? What is below the window? What torment will assail my ears the next morning? What is the bed like? Will my back survive the night?

Well, you can calm yourself down with certain routines. You can take with you some beloved objects from home, wind up your own alarm-clock, light a candle you have brought with you, open a longed-for book . . . anything to avoid thinking about the state of your throat, to avoid remembering that it functions best if the person in whom it is situated is as comfortable as possible.

If that person cannot cope with the switch to another climate and different surroundings, that means finding a good throat-specialist. Innumerable are those patient silent men who have looked down my throat and painted, sprayed and irradiated the area round those unfortunate little threads called vocal cords. They know as well as I do that the only things that help are silence, rest and warmth, and they also know that it is no use saying that to an artist who in

62

an hour or two will be facing an expectant audience and forcing herself to appear fresh, well and rested. So together we devote ourselves to a mass of hocus-pocus to create that illusion. It usually works, oddly enough. But it is hard on the nerves.

The strangest treatment I have ever had was in Tashkent. I was quite hoarse after travelling from wintry Europe to a hot oriental climate. After the first night's performance of *Traviata*, they took me to the hospital. A smiling little woman doctor greeted me with the words: 'Welcome! When I heard you in Act IV last night, I thought: I'm almost sure to be seeing her tomorrow.' She consoled me and said she would fix things, then took me into a room with small booths screened off with white sheets. Small veiled nurses brought out a large electrical apparatus, placed a pad on my throat, another at the back of my neck, and through my interpreter explained that they were now going to pass an electric current through my neck. Would I please indicate when things began to flicker before my eyes. After a while I screamed 'now', at which they smiled again and made signs that I should sit like that for twelve minutes. Then I was left alone. My terror grew and I was convinced my last hour had come. Hysteria was at its peak when I suddenly heard someone clearing his throat on the other side of the sheet. I pulled it aside and there, my goodness, was my Alfredo from the night before. He was receiving the same treatment, and that made me feel better. Whether the treatment had any effect whatsoever or whether I simply got better on my own, I simply don't know, but anyhow, the following night I sang Marguerite in *Faust* without any disasters.

Going to a strange hairdresser is another complication. Every country and every hairdresser has his or her own idea of what a concert-singer should look like. Trying to persuade an unknown hairdresser to do exactly the style you want yourself all too often strains your patience and takes up far too much of that precious energy you need to carry out your work on the platform. Sitting with wet hair among chattering smoking customers in a salon of buzzing hair-dryers is an enervating prelude to a concert. Perhaps one should try using wigs more often.

I sometimes take electric curlers with me and try to do my own hair. That is when you discover how many kinds of wall-sockets there are in the world. As one cannot rely on the apparatus working, it is better to do battle with a hairdresser who insists on 'soft curls', which you know after ten minutes on the platform in the excitement that warms your body, will look as if you have just come straight from a shower.

A woman travelling alone also involves going to eat in restaurants alone. It always amuses me immensely to watch the head-waiter's reaction when a woman comes in and says she is alone. Even if there are twenty empty tables by the window or in other pleasant places, you are nevertheless always taken to an odd small table next to the kitchen entrance or by the door to the cloakroom. For the first ten years of my travelling life, I never dared protest, but I am braver now and ignore the disapproval I meet when I say I do not want to sit there. I promise to eat expensively and quickly, but I wish to sit in a nice place while I do so.

Organisers often meet you with flowers in their hands at airports or stations. Friendliness and heart-warming thoughtfulness accompany you right through rehearsals and performances, and you are invited to a good supper after the performance.

Then the next morning when you leave the place, everyone has vanished. No one worries about whether you get up in time for the first morning train or plane, and the number of times you succeed in acquiring a cup of coffee to revive you after the strains of the night before is very few. *Sic transit Gloria Swanson,* as I usually say. There is nothing so unglamorous in the world as the artist the day after with her bouquet of flowers wrapped in newspaper, dragging her suitcase along the station platform at seven o'clock in the morning.

One nightmare is finding yourself alone in a hotel on a Friday night, perhaps hungry and tired, and then finding that it is 'dancing tonight', which usually means no meals can be served in your room. To guard against this, I have often bought provisions in the afternoon, and then I not only have something to eat, but also manage to avoid invitations as a handy 'lone woman' dance-partner.

During a tour in Sweden, the company was standing shivering one cold winter morning on the station in Falköping. I was calling down curses on to a brutal world that could not provide me with a hot drink before taking my sensitive throat out into this hostile climate. No porters and not a soul who understood you might need some help humping a heavy case up on to that uncomfortable rail-bus with room in it for neither people nor luggage. 'And why does the damned thing never stop where I'm standing. And what's all the hurry . . . ?'

But I got up in the end and the rail-bus rattled off. The guard made his way towards me. 'Now he's going to tell me I can't stand here. But I *won't* move. I'll be *sick* if I have to go into that hot crowded compartment.'

The guard saluted and said : 'Miss Söderström, could you possibly go up front to the driver and speak to him. You see, you're one of his greatest favourites. He likes you because you're always so nice and friendly.'

Guess who was ashamed.

# 10/ Doesn't Anything Happen on the Stage?

In interviews, the question 'Doesn't anything happen on the stage?' is always cropping up.

What do they mean by 'happen'? In this respect, these reporters, if I may put it this way, are typical representatives of an average audience, who think it is exciting and amusing if something goes wrong during a performance. When I finally realised this fact, a great deal of my nervousness left me and my profession became easier. I found I could perform in a more relaxed way.

Certainly things that have not been reckoned with often do happen. One of the more drastic misfortunes I have been involved in on the stage was during a performance of Offenbach's *La Belle Hélène* at the Opera House in Stockholm. The bed in Hélène's boudoir was shaped like a great shell and covered with shining slippery pink satin. Very beautiful.

'The most beautiful woman in the world' sings a couplet that runs: 'Tell me, Venus, tell me, are such things right for a royal personage.' At the end of the last verse is a piquant little addition, and to give a little extra zest to the polish of the couplet, the choreographer had instituted a small routine that always brought applause. Hélène lies down on her back at the end of the shell-bed, bends her head back over the edge so that she is eye to eye with the audience, then flings her legs up in an elegant pose as she simultaneously spreads out her arms.

We performed night after night, and I grew bolder and bolder. One night, I abandoned all caution when it came to finding some support for my shoulders as I threw myself down on the bed, and I just flung myself carelessly backward —elegantly, I thought . . . missed, and did a back-somersault over the edge of the bed, then another back-somersault down the steps of the platform the whole structure was standing on, landing in a final pose slap in front of the prompter's box, my wig awry and my legs wide apart. I was, however, sufficiently conscious to be able to complete my lines: 'Now I feel strong enough to meet him!'

'Him' was Per Grundén, who was standing in the wings waiting for his entrance. He did not bother to go on stage for a long while, because he was convinced I had passed out and we would have to bring down the curtain. But strangely enough, I was quite unhurt and the performance came to an end as usual. Afterwards, some friends of mine from America on a visit to Stockholm came to see me in my dressing-room. They were enormously impressed. 'Do you really do that trick every night?' It would have been foolish of me not to lay it on a little thick. 'Of course!' They were leaving the next day, so could not check, and a little extra publicity on the US jungle-telegraph would do no harm.

I remember with horror the first time I ever played Sophie in *Der Rosenkavalier*, at the Metropolitan Opera in New York. I had sung both the Marschallin and Octavian before and was anticipating with some trepidation the problem that would arise when I tried to sing in another voice in the intricate ensembles. The rehearsals were even more difficult as my fellow-singers were of the prima-donna variety who did not wish to tire their throats before the performance, and there I was, singing Sophie outwardly, but inwardly singing all the other parts, for I knew them all.

The night of the performance arrived and to say the least of it, I was terrified, as I still had not had a chance to see whether I could stick to my new line when the others were singing my previous rôles all round me. An added reason for my nervousness was that the performance was being broadcast to an audience calculated to be about ten million listeners. Pity if I went wrong . . .

The dress I was to wear was of heavy silk, a splendid crinoline, which I am sure looked very romantic from the auditorium, but which weighed at least twenty pounds. As if in a dream, I heard the overture to the second act, the curtain went up to reveal for the first time Sophie-Elisabeth, who took a deep breath and tried to produce a teenage girl's trembling excitement in face of Rosenkavalier's arrival. It went quite well and my voice obeyed me.

You may think what you like about Strauss' music, but he is undeniably one of the very few composers who really can build up an entrance. The festive fanfare-like chords that bring Octavian on to the stage always send shivers of delight down my spine whenever I hear them. It was the same this time, too, as I, as Sophie for the time being, sank into a low curtsey.

My dress was of strong air-tight material, and the crinoline acted just like a suction-cup. As I curtseyed, the air was pressed out and fifty beats later, when I tried to rise to my feet, the weight of the dress was unexpectedly great, my calf-muscles locked themselves into cramp and I simply could not get up. My leg hurt, my head felt quite numbed, and somewhere in the distance I could hear music that I vaguely recognised, but my whole being was filled with one single thought: 'I must get up.' Every effort was in vain, and in the end, with my Octavian staring in confusion at this

68

peculiar Sophie, who received the rose sitting on the floor, I hissed between my teeth: 'Help!', smelt the rose in my hand and repeated: 'Help!'

Not until the whole enchanting scene of the handing over of the rose and the duet that follows were over, did the others round me realise that there was something wrong with Sophie. Who knows . . . Scandinavian singers have a style of their own in opera, haven't they, and as we had had no proper rehearsals, how could they know that this was not the way I had thought of playing the scene?

Octavian and Marianne helped me to my feet again, the cramp loosened and the rest of the opera continued normally. My first question when the curtain went down was of course: 'Did I sing?', and I was very relieved when they replied: 'Sure, your phrases came where they should, which was why we thought you wanted to sit on the floor.'

In another performance of *Der Rosenkavalier*, I sang Octavian with Elizabeth Schwarzkopf, one of the artists I most admire and from whom I have learnt a great deal. She was making a guest appearance in Stockholm as the Marschallin in our production. She had brought her own costumes with her, which entailed that in the first act she appeared in a romantic chiffon nightdress, over which she then swiftly flung a lovely négligée of taffeta. This négligée was fastened to the edge of the nightdress with a long row of press-studs. The dresser in the wings had not had a chance to see how this worked and in her haste and nervousness in the brief moments available, she started with the wrong press-stud and so the whole garment was skew-whiff, as they say.

When the Marschallin rushed in to reproach Octavian, her head was right down in her décolletage and her hands were occupied with unfastening the press-studs and trying to do them up again. I saw her problem, and gripped with a strong desire to help our cherished guest, I abandoned my rehearsed scenes and made my way to her side as often as I could. Tenderly, I put my arm round her shoulders and pressed a stud here and a stud there. It took time, because Octavian has to carry out a number of other actions in this scene, and when Baron Ochs is present, Octavian must not be exposed by touching his 'mistress'. So the covert little movements were spread out all through the first act. When the curtain went down, however, the whole négligée was in place.

This incident is evidence that misfortune on the stage can sometimes be used to advantage. Afterwards, we heard how wonderful it had been to see the fine relationship we had between us. The tenderness I had shown for Marie-Therèse with my small almost unnoticeable caresses had been quite irresistible.

Clothes can be the cause of a great deal of misery on the stage, and one is always haunted by the thought of losing a skirt because hooks and eyes burst when singing muscles are brought into action. So dressers often put in extra safety-pins to guard against such misfortune.

In *Madame Butterfly*, I had a complicated construction of Japanese garments that tended to go askew whenever I moved quickly across the stage or fell to my knees. So my beloved worried dresser one evening put some extra-large safety-pins at the back to ensure that the huge bow really would stay in place all through the second act. Full of confidence, I went on stage and the curtains flew apart. So did the safety-pins in my back, the very first time I rose to my feet. The scenes for Butterfly in this act might be described as highly energetic housewifely-gymnastics and carrying out these movements with pins sticking in my back is something I shall never forget. If it had been comedy, I could easily have found an opportunity to put a hand under my dress to get hold of those sharp pins. But this was profound tragedy, so all I could do was to carry on.

Clothes can also be very distracting, as can be shown from a concert performance of Verdi's *Requiem* I was taking part in. It was the last of three concerts, and every night a wonderful ensemble had given a whole new dimension to this work, one I love very much. We had a Bulgarian bass, who sounded so superb in the *Agnus Dei* that one simply melted. On the last night, when we came to it, I settled down on my chair, closed my eyes and prepared to enjoy it. He did not come in on his cue. I opened my eyes and saw this usually confident colleague of mine trying to find his place in the music. After a few bars, he was back again, but the tone in his voice was strained.

After the concert, we all rushed up to him. 'What happened? Were you feeling ill?' 'No, I just happened to glance down at my feet as I was getting ready to sing the *Agnus Dei*, and I saw that I was wearing red socks instead of my black stockings. Red socks . . . well, that wasn't all that terrible. But then I started wondering where I had put the black ones.'

Stepping into a production that you have never seen, without any rehearsals, is very difficult indeed. I try to avoid such engagements, but sometimes one is forced to, as for instance when I was touring the USSR. The last performance I did there was *Faust* at the Kirov Opera House in Leningrad, a beautiful theatre in a dreamy beautiful city. I had been touring all round the country for two weeks, singing the same part in several other places, and I had found out that sometimes the performance ended with the prison scene, and sometimes with the Walpurgis act.

In Leningrad, I was given a short run-through in a room

with the producer, and we discussed the scenes with some of my colleagues present. I was trying to manage without an interpreter, and I asked how they ended the opera here? In the prison. Oh yes. When Mefisto sings 'she is damned', you fall down on the floor, facing the audience. Then as the chorus sings 'she is saved', a group of nuns come on and you get up facing the audience. Then a 'blahblahblah' comes up to you and places a hand on your shoulder.

I had never heard this word before, but I presumed it probably meant an abbess, so I said, all right, yes. And then you go off into the wings and the curtain goes down. Right, I said.

The evening arrived. It was a fantastic experience to be on this stage that I had heard and read so much about, and I did my very best to give an acceptable interpretation that I had improvised to a great extent for that night. Everything went well and we got successfully through to the end. After my last note and Mefisto's curse, I threw myself face down into the straw in the prison. The chorus sang: 'She is saved', and I got to my knees, a blissful smile on my face. I went on looking blissful as I sensed a group of people approaching from behind me, the nuns. I rose to my feet and suddenly felt a powerful hand falling on my shoulder. Damned strong abbess, I had time to think, before turning round to be confronted with the scarlet mask of the executioner on a man six foot tall with a gigantic sword in his hand.

In all previous productions of *Faust*, I had always floated up some steps that led to an allegorical end-station in heaven, so I was utterly unprepared for the shock I received when I realised that this Marguerite really was going to be executed, and I was very lucky that the supernumerary who had the part of the executioner was so strong that with that grip on my shoulder, he really could drag me off the stage.

# 11/ Television—A New Medium

When my father was sixty years old, his friends gave him a television set. It stood like a dark, silent, alien creature in the corner of my parents' living-room, a creature that could neither speak nor communicate in any other way. That was in 1950.

When the first experimental broadcasts gradually began to appear, this apparatus suddenly became an attraction. Friends and neighbours were invited to pleasant little gatherings around the brief moments when the box in the corner came to life, and the evening when the daughter of the house appeared on the screen, my father wept great tears of joy at being allowed to experience such a miracle.

Naturally, I thought it very exciting to be in on the beginnings of this medium in this way. I have always thought it much more rewarding to spend time on pioneer work than to trudge along ready-made tracks.

In 1954, I did my first opera on television. I was invited by Herbert Sandberg to take part in Leo Blech's opera *Versiegelt* (Sealed), and worked for a few weeks in the studios in Lokstedt in Hamburg, next door to the Hagenbeck Zoo. This was considered very practical, because the zoo-keepers could be used to control the wild opera-artists when they became troublesome.

I had tried films before, and that had not suited me at all.

Filming short scenes with no kind of connection between them, and then taking them again from different angles and getting up at five o'clock to do so . . . I simply couldn't cope. In television, on the other hand, you could combine the advantage of being able to play with fine nuances and mime, with the enjoyment of playing a rôle from start to finish. That went considerably better. I at once felt at home in front of the television cameras.

The first opera broadcast in Sweden occurred the same year. Mozart's *Bastien and Bastienne* was broadcast from Drottningholm Theatre and it did not seem anything remarkable to us, as we performed it as we usually did. The intimate surroundings in that beautiful old theatre are said to have added to the success of the broadcast, which went out on Eurovision.

Gradually, studio productions of operas started and Blomdahl's *Aniara* spaceship was built in the great studios in Valhalla Road. For everyone involved, it was an unforgettable occasion. Technical difficulties were clearly very great and rehearsals and recordings dragged on, so in the end we felt barricaded in for ever . . . whether in a space-ship in space, or in a studio in Valhalla Road, it did not seem to matter as they ran into night and then into day again and all sense of time and space vanished.

Arne Arnbom, the visionary pioneer of opera and classical music on television in Sweden, produced another broadcast that also had its highlights. It was a bold conception, a production of Puccini's opera *Il Tabarro* (The Cloak), the action of which takes place on a barge on the banks of the Seine.

We were going to play it on a barge, indeed yes, but on the banks of Lake Karlberg, where there were ideal facilities for placing all the cameras at our disposal—was it two, or three?

At first, we rehearsed in the studio and then on board the barge. It was the beginning of May and cool, to say the least of it. But we consoled ourselves that it would be much warmer by the fifteenth of May, when it was to be broadcast.

On the morning of the fifteenth of May, it was snowing. The snow gradually changed to pouring rain. Telephone messages went round in the morning to everyone taking part. The broadcast would probably be postponed, but stay at home. At four o'clock, the rain stopped. Another message: 'We're going on. Come down to the barge for make-up.'

So I was transformed into a beautiful curly-haired Giorgetta, wife of the barge-owner and lover of one of the stevedores on board. The opera is a passionate drama of jealousy that ends with the skipper-husband by chance giving the lover-stevedore the secret signal he is waiting for to come to that night's lover's meeting with Giorgetta. When the Skipper strikes a match to light his pipe, the lover thinks it is Giorgetta giving him the all clear, and he creeps on board straight into the arms of the husband. The husband draws a knife and stabs the lover to death, and hides the corpse beneath his cloak. Giorgetta hears the noise and comes up on deck, where the tragedy ends the moment the husband flings open his cloak and shows her that her secret love is over.

The opera begins with a line of men carrying the barge's cargo of sacks ashore. 'Such terrible heat,' sang our artists, as they wiped their foreheads and their freezing breath came billowing out of their mouths like smoke. Slightly later in the opera, the two lovers are standing by the railing, planning how to meet alone again. The iron railing was icy cold and when my bare arms just touched it, I jumped.

After twenty minutes broadcasting, it began to rain, and as the drama progressed, the more dramatic we looked.

75

Straggly wet strands of hair hung round our faces, helping to give us expressions of desperation that we could never have dreamt of achieving. We were not only drenched in the sounds from the Radio Orchestra, which excelled itself under Nils Grevillius' direction, but also by a May downpour that was offering the tragedy unexpected assistance.

Among other television broadcasts was a musical entertainment broadcast by the BBC direct from London. The whole thing began for me by finding no taxi at the station and so taking the underground, getting out at the wrong station and becoming completely lost, lugging a large suitcase full of dresses. Finally, I got a lift in the only vehicle in sight, a huge road-sweeper, and thus arrived at Maida Vale studios, to be received by a gold-bespattered commissionaire, who in the best British tradition merely raised his eyebrows a trifle when I announced that I was the Star of the Eric Robinson Show.

In the first part of the programme, I was to sing the waltz aria from Gounod's *Romeo and Juliet*. The great studio was divided up into four. A large part was taken up with space for a ballet duo, one corner was for Geza Anda and his grand piano, a whole scene had been constructed for the final opera extract, and then there was a small corner for me to stand in and sing my aria. The orchestra was in a neighbouring studio and could only be heard through loudspeakers. It was quite tricky singing to that accompaniment, but Eric Robinson knew the art of following you with his orchestra.

Just before we were due to go on, the woman producer, Paddy Foy, came into the make-up room to see me. 'The programme's a bit short. Elisabeth, dear, could you sing an extra number? What about one of those Swedish unaccompanied songs you told us about?'

'Of course I can. Almquist ...?'

'Great! And you'll translate the words for us, won't you? 'Bye-bye, good luck.'

I had just time to think out that I would choose *Why Did You Come to the Meadow*, when it was time to get dressed and go out into the studio. I forgot to ask anyone where they had thought the extra song should go in the programme.

I am standing in front of the camera, the studio-man gives a sign, the red light on the camera goes on, and in through the door comes Eric Robinson and stands beside me. 'Hullo, Elisabeth, how nice to see you here.' He asks me what I'm doing and I answer nicely, while at the back of my mind I'm thinking: 'If he's going to stand beside me, that means I have to start without accompaniment until he has time to get back to the orchestra.' So when Eric asks me: 'Now, what are we going to hear you sing?' I have thought up a witty introduction to my song and answer by asking him if he is interested in growing roses. With a bewildered expression, Eric says yes, indeed he is, but why? 'Well,' I go on bravely. 'Would you like to sleep on a bed of roses?'

'I think you should sing your aria now,' says Eric, and through the loudspeakers, I hear the short prelude to the waltz aria, at which I instinctively draw breath and set off on the chromatic scale that introduces the song. Meanwhile, I see Eric creeping out. I sing the whole aria without really knowing what I'm doing. When the aria comes to an end, the red lamp just goes on shining red. I stare like a large question-mark at the studio-man behind the camera, and he waves at me to go on, so I smile straight into the camera and go on, saying tentatively: 'And now ladies and gentlemen, I would like to sing a little Swedish song for you.' The studio-man nods mutely in agreement and signals 'increase tempo.'

'*Hvarför kom du hit i kväll*—Why did you come here

77

tonight—*jag kom hit att träffa dig*—I came to see you—*går du åter bort ikväll säg*—are you leaving me tonight—*nej jag går ej bort från dig*—no I won't leave you (this is going fine) *blir du hela natten kvar säg*—are you staying all the night— *jag blir kvar i natt hos dig*—I'll stay with you all night. *Nu skola vi våra vålmar* . . . um . . . er . . . um (what on earth is *vålmar* in English—I'll skip over it)—and now let us, let us, rake hay, yes, and cut roses, and make a bed of roses and then (no, I can't cope any longer) have fun on that bed!'

By this time I was feeling like a boiled lobster. The camera-man had let go the camera and was holding his hand over his mouth, and the studio-man was doubled up in paroxysms of laughter, stuffing the corner of his jacket into his mouth to suppress them. However, for two difficult minutes, I managed to get through *Why Did You Come to the Meadow* for the first time on British television.

This experience came in useful back home in Sweden, because one night when I was taking part in a chat-programme, I told listeners and viewers about these agonies of mine and from an entertainment point of view they went down very well indeed.

# 12/ Concerts

Concert seasons are arranged very far in advance. When you are standing on a platform one evening in April, 1978, you sometimes wonder how on earth you could have been so over-optimistic, or rather foolish, to have put together the difficult and demanding programme you are about to per-form. At the end of a long and intensive season like this, it seems over-ambitious and insurmountable. And then you remember one sunny day in July, 1976, a leafy garden, a comfortable chair and a gin and tonic with ice tinkling in it. Out of a cloudless sky come all the most beautiful songs in the world—you think of the huge wealth of marvellous music and wonder what Wolf would sound like after Schubert, then the added piquancy of Strauss, then French songs, and wonderful Liszt, and the Russian songs, and Swedish, of course, and then Kilpinen and Grieg, of course . . .

So you write down your thoughts and some six months later, that letter has gone through impresarios and concert managements, while you yourself have hardly given it another thought, because so much else is happening that you have to put your mind to. Proofs of programmes arrive and you put them in the pile of future engagements. Then the day before the concert arrives and you are faced with the fact that these are the songs the audience is expecting to hear and you begin to see the extent of the work ahead of you.

I have a dream. I would like to have a brochure printed of all the songs I know, by now about three hundred. They would be numbered. Then I would join up with a good and understanding accompanist and spend the rest of my life doing concerts like this: when I have accepted an engagement, I would tell the organisers that the programme will be announced from the platform on the evening. Then we would come in with all the music and only the first song would be decided beforehand.

When you have sung one song, you already know what kind of audience you have in front of you, and you also know the kind of music they would prefer to listen to. Then I would be able to say: 'Now I'll sing number twenty-four, and after that number seventy-three . . .' The audience could choose something from the printed repertoire. Why not? They should have some say in the matter, too. After all, laws have now been passed in Sweden that everyone shall have a say in decisions.

When I was about five years old, my father took me to a concert. Later on, I was told that it was Kirsten Flagstad who was singing in the Concert Hall's large auditorium, but what I remember from that occasion is not a great voice or a musical experience. I remember the lady in a blue dress and a large diamond ring that glittered, sending sharp rays of light into my eyes. That in itself was quite useful, because I also remember that I kept getting terribly sleepy, but woke up whenever that light shone in my eyes.

After many years of appearing in concerts, I have found that when I return to a place a few years later and meet someone who was at my last concert there, I often hear: 'I so well remember that lovely pink dress you were wearing three years ago.' 'Oh, do you? What did I sing then?' 'Oh, well, you know, I just can't remember.'

I think this is a very interesting phenomenon, and it makes me be careful to keep track of what I wear at concerts. Sing the same songs over and over again, by all means, but it is mortal sin to appear in the same dress twice!

My first concert gowns were a matter of chance, depending on what Holmblom's shop in Stureplan in Stockholm had in their sale. Once a year, one could buy real bargains at a third of their original price. So I became the owner of a fabulous dress of heavy white silk, covered with white tulle, embroidered in lovely patterns with pearls of emerald green, olive green, blue silver and lilac. Whenever I went on to the platform in that dress, a great sigh went through the audience.

That was a wonderful concert gown and also it did not need ironing. When it was fashionable to have great wide tulle skirts, this was indeed an added advantage. Oh, the hours spent ironing miles of tulle of all colours! Wearying of that, once again I fell for a tight sheath dress of yellow lace, an elegant garment that made me look as slim as a mannequin. The first time I wore it was in the concert-hall in Gothenburg, where the route from the wings to where I was to stand and sing on the platform was quite long. In that narrow dress, it seemed endless. I could take only small tripping steps, which was almost certainly an added reason why the audience brought me back again and again, as I think it amused them to see my mincing gait.

When I was to sing in the Albert Hall in London for the first time, I had just had a child and was what you might call rather broad in the beam. Despite this, I chose a narrow red brocade dress that made me look very slim . . . from the front. The rehearsals with the orchestra took place in another hall, and so I had not seen the platform until I made my entrance that evening. In I marched in a cheerful mood, with the knowledge that only the orchestra would see my broad behind. I greeted the audience and then turned to greet the orchestra. Then I noticed . . . several hundred people were sitting behind me, as the hall is like a circus. Instinctively, I put my hands over the most exposed part of my anatomy, and sang most of the programme that way. But it all went quite well, for there is simply no audience in the world as stimulating as Prom audiences in the Albert Hall.

If a concert has been successful, occasionally you imagine that your clothes have brought you luck, and you get enormously attached to a particular garment. I had a 'lucky' dress like that and I loved it so much that it was only with great strength of mind I could part with it. It had a loose covering of pink chiffon with great hand-painted butterflies on it, which you could have at the front or back. Whichever way you wore it, it hid the unattractive apparatus for singing, and you felt beautiful although you had to take deep breaths that made your diaphragm expand several centimetres.

When I was touring the United States, giving concerts of romantic songs, I often found that the very first questions I was asked when the organisers met me at the airport were: 'What are you going to wear? Do you change in the interval?' They always insisted that you rehearsed entrances and exits very thoroughly, so that the artist was properly lit. They also put down special carpets on the platform so that your dress would not get dirty! I had a very smart dress made for me for these concerts. It was made of organdie with a wide white skirt comprising four layers of material. The bodice was white with no shoulder-straps, the top part white organdie, but it also had a wide sash of dark-blue silk. With this went a skirt of the same blue silk, and you could fasten that over the white dress. I began the concert by appearing in the blue dress with white embellishments, and after the interval when I had taken off the top skirt, I appeared thus in a white dress with blue embellishments. It was an ingenious but sophisticated affair that worked wonderfully and I grieved when it finally wore out.

Once when I was in the audience in Edinburgh at a concert at which a famous international singer was performing, I went behind the scenes during the interval to speak to one of the organisers. The first half of the concert had been somewhat confusing, as the artists had changed the programme without warning the audience, and I had a feeling some more surprises were on the way.

I met the director of the festival in the corridor behind the platform. His hair was on end and there was a slightly insane look in his eyes. 'Elisabeth, my dear, could you go into Madame immediately. I've just come from there. I think she's on her way home. She's got undressed. What's she going to do?'

I knocked on the door of the artist's room and stepped inside. I thanked her for the first half of the programme and said I was looking forward to the second half . . .'I'm going to hear it, aren't I?' 'Of course,' said Madame. 'Why not?' 'Well, the organisers are a bit frightened that you're leaving, as you've got undressed.' 'Not at all. But my dress is so grand and expensive, I didn't want to spoil it by sitting down in it.'

When you come to a new place and sing for the first time in a concert-hall, it is very tempting to try out the acoustics. Ah, what an illusion! You can go and look at the colour of the background so that you don't choose a dress that clashes with it, and you can try out colours and positions of spotlights. But never, never imagine you know anything about what it will sound like later on in the evening.

Rehearsing in an empty concert-hall is very exhilarating. 'Oh, don't I sound good, and how marvellously it resounds. How easy it is to sing here.' When the evening comes and you step out into a full hall and sing your first note, with horror you think: 'I've lost my voice. It didn't sound like that this morning. I *have* lost my voice.' Beads of sweat appear and it takes a long time to adjust your senses to the different acoustics, but with the help of the audience's reactions, you realise that perhaps they can hear you after all. Never rehearse in an empty hall!

# 13/ Golden Moments

When I think back on my life, there are golden moments that I enjoy living through again, remembering them almost physically. Some of them are in connection with Jussi Björling. The first time I sang with him was in Puccini's *Manon Lescaut*.

I had been hearing him on the gramophone ever since childhood. He was one of my father's great idols, and together we had seen him perform in *Tosca* and *Bohème*. Now I was standing beside him and he was supposed to be the fiery young Des Grieux, besotted with his love for Manon. My reverence for him was deep-rooted and so I kept using his title of Court Singer, or else Mr Björling, not Jussi. We had not had many rehearsals, and had gone almost straight into performance.

It was said that Jussi did not act well. Maybe he did not physically express the rôle he was interpreting, but I was surprised to find that he could transform himself into exactly the person I wanted Des Grieux to be, with his eyes and the intensity he put into every word and note. Right through the whole performance, he lived the part, and for me, who suffer when people turn private on the stage, this was tremendous.

And then that voice pouring out so freely—suddenly I

85

felt all the tensions in my own throat relax; an intoxicating sense of freedom made me sing as I had never sung before. Jussi's notes struck me quite physically and I felt released.

When we were facing the audience after the last act, receiving the applause, I plucked up courage and whispered : 'Please can I use your Christian name, Mr Björling?' At which Jussi gave me a hug in front of all those people and said: 'My dear girl, I've been waiting for that all evening.'

The next time I sang with Jussi was in New York, where he was making a come-back after several years' absence. I was singing Marguerite in Gounod's *Faust* for the first time in my life, and I went to the theatre that night with terror in my heart and my limbs trembling. We had had only one run-through with the orchestra and scenery, and I was not sufficiently prepared. I said so to Jussi, and looking at me with compassion, he said: 'My dear young friend, you've nothing to be afraid of. Not many people are making demands on you yet. It's much worse for me, because they're all waiting to see if I'm finished, or whether I can live up to my reputation.'

Despite his usual calm tone of voice, I could hear the anxiety that every mature artist feels before going on stage. 'As long as I can do what they expect of me!'

In 1960, I was appearing as guest artist with Stockholm Opera in London, and the night after the last performance, I took a flight to Geneva. There I took a train to Montreux, and tired and shaken on my arrival, I took a taxi to the hotel and fell headlong into bed for a few hours' sleep before going to a rehearsal. When the telephone woke me, I had not the slightest idea where I was. A giant bed in a large room, the ceiling of which was very high. Thick red velvet curtains. I got up and went over to the curtains, which I thought were drawn across the window. When I drew them back, I found

86

two large balcony doors and I opened them . . . and there was the Lake of Geneva with the whole range of the Alps behind it in glittering sunlight.

It took a long time before I realised I was not dreaming. When I was rehearsing Mozart's *Vesperae Solennae* later on, in my inner vision I kept seeing the brilliantly white crystal-glitter of Mont Blanc. Ever since then, the Alps have always been inextricably linked with Mozart in my mind. Mont Blanc definitely looks as a Mozart symphony sounds. These combinations of worlds of beauty gave me a vision of how I would look on life from then on.

That day, the newspapers reported that Jussi Björling was dead.

When I was at opera school, I was an extra the night Birgit Nilsson was making her début as Lady Macbeth. I remember the exalted atmosphere both on the stage and in the audience. Everyone felt this was an historic occasion, one of the greatest singers of the century beginning her career. I was very impressed, but it was not until later that I was so deeply moved by Birgit's voice.

This occurred during a performance of *The Valkyrie*, in which I stood with all the other Amazons on a rock with shield, lance, helmet, cloak and all the other attributes which made life on that rock a case for safety-at-work regulations, though they had not been invented then. We were totally occupied trying to survive stumbling about in the semi-dark-ness on a grass-covered wooden frame that was supposed to be the Valkyrie rock. Long skirts and high boots made it very difficult to move and then we also had to sing as well, prefer-ably in the places Wagner had intended.

Then Brünnhilde and Sieglinde come on and at the end of their scene there is a wonderful phrase in which Sieglinde sings *O sel'ge Wonne*. When Birgit sang that phrase my

87

whole body went doiinngg! I had never before heard such an overwhelming, warm, beautiful and mighty flood of sound at such close quarters. It was and is still marvellous, and more than anything else evidence that singing can affect the listener purely physically.

The first time I myself felt the intoxication of my own voice as a natural force pouring out of my throat and bursting all limits that singing techniques and other inhibitions can put on you, was in Orff's *Carmina Burana*. The soprano's last contribution is a long cadenza-like melody, *Dulcissime totam tibi subdo me* (With the greatest sweetness I give myself to thee) and then the whole chorus comes in with the great final chorus of *O Fortuna*.

How can I describe the ecstasy you feel when every fibre in your body vibrates on the same wavelength as the notes, when a high C-sharp suddenly sparkles in front of you as if a sun had appeared in the auditorium . . .

My own sense of happiness seemed to be infectious, because the audience was 'struck' just as forcibly as I was myself, and Hans Schmidt-Isserstedt, who was conducting, called me *Dolcissima* from that day on. When my first child was born, he re-baptized me to *Dolcissimama*.

As early as in 1948 when I sang Anna in *Värmlänningarna* (The People of Värmland) by F. R. Dahlgren, I had been involved in the wonderful experience when an auditorium full of people hold its breath together with the artist. Anna has fainted in church, is carried outside, and slowly emerges from her terrible dream in which she has heard the banns confirmed between Erik, her lover, and Britta: 'Her not me'. And Anna slowly slips into 'confusion of mind' as she sings farewell to her love: 'Goodnight, now, thou my darling friend.'

When I had sung the last note in this most melancholy

song and was sitting there until the curtain came down, the audience was deathly silent. Then I heard the first sob and someone blew a nose and someone else in the auditorium cleared a throat. I was filled with an astonishing flood of emotion. 'They're crying for me, for my Anna.' It was wonderful.

In my experience, I am usually so absorbed in the rôle I am playing when the curtain goes down, I don't really register what is happening when they push you out to receive the applause. I plod out and back again as if in a fog, and I don't wake up until I am back in my dressing-room. But I do remember very well what it was like the first time I had to go out front at the Met to take what is called a solo curtain-call. I was completely unprepared for the sound of four thousand people at once airing their delight and calling bravo. I reacted as if someone had pushed me backwards, but it was very stimulating! It is only a pity that one becomes blasé so soon, and it wasn't long before I took it as quite natural that it should sound like the world ice-hockey championships every time I showed myself.

I have a truly golden memory from the Royal Opera's guest appearance at the Palace of Versailles, where we performed *Orfeo* by Gluck in the palace theatre. This has been restored, but it is very beautiful all the same, and it made an appropriate setting for our performance, which is done in magnificent baroque costumes.

After the performance, all the great palace rooms were *illuminées* and the audience was able to walk round their brilliantly lit splendour to see how festive it looked in candlelight. We were also allowed to do this, but to save time we were asked to keep our costumes on and go straight from the stage. There is a great number of mirrors in these palace rooms, and it was quite extraordinary to see yourself

D

and your colleagues in those handsome costumes in those surroundings. The heavy silks and velvets with their extravagant decorations in gold and silver thread seemed to have been made to melt in with the décor. We walked with dignified steps through salon after salon, and gradually we were transformed from people of today and visiting artists into the rightful inhabitants of the palace.

When the promenade was over, the lights extinguished, and we had to start changing and taking off our make-up, we felt as if we had been awakened out of a dream, or like children who have had their toys taken away from them.

Another walk I shall never forget was one I made for one of the Prima Primadonna programmes for television. I very much wanted to sing an aria from Bellini's *The Sleepwalker*. I had been attracted to it as a child and had always loved it. My mother often used to play it in a piano arrangement by Thalberg.

But . . . how to catch the interest of the viewer with romantic nineteenth century music? I wrote on the manuscript: 'We must have such exciting pictures here that people who don't like this kind of music will still go on watching.' I had long discussions with Kjerstin Dellert and Bo Billtén about where our sleepwalker's walk should take place. In the end, the uppermost balustrade of the Opera House was decided on. 'Elisabeth walks in her sleep on top of the Opera House.' What a headline!

In a violet-coloured chiffon dress, in the middle of October, when it was so cold the cameramen's hands could hardly cope with the cameras, I walked along the balustrade, while the producer, the script-holder, technicians, attendants, the lights-boys, and everyone else involved in television filmmaking all sat on the sloping metal roof, holding their breath. A breathtakingly beautiful view out over Stockholm at least made me forget my giddiness and vertigo. At first I wore a belt with a safety-line fastened to it underneath my dress. But I felt as if I would be dragged down by the weight of the rope, so after a while I unhooked it.

When the programme was broadcast, we had several tele-phone calls and letters from people who had bets on whether I was really up there or whether the film had been faked. Dear people, I assure you it was only too real, and yet when I walk down in Gustaf Adolf Square below and look upwards, I cannot really believe that it was true that we played that scene right up there.

In another of the Primadonna programmes, Kjerstin and I wanted to be allowed to sing the Barcarolle from *The Tales* of *Hoffmann* sitting in one of the green fishing-boats in the Stream in Stockholm. And it was arranged! Not without some difficulty, as there had to be a police-guard, and the sluice-gates had to be closed, and there had to be a boatload of frogmen in case we fell into the water, and so on and so forth.

After a thousand sorrows and eight afflictions, as we say in Swedish, the filming took place, and when the Barcarolle scene was over, to the notes of *To Sea*, with Carl Milles' Sun-Singer statue as décor, we glided down Stockholm Stream. Then the spotlights went out and we were rowed slowly back to the quay. At midnight, in romantic dark-blue wraps, slowly being rowed in a green fishing-boat from the Royal Palace up Stockholm Stream to the Royal Opera House, with the full moon shining down on the Sun-Singer . . . that really was another golden moment.

One winter's evening after a long day in the television studios with the Primadonnas, Kjerstin Dellert and I went to Stockholm Concert Hall to listen to Isaac Stern giving a violin recital, arriving just as the second half was starting.

We sank into our seats, relishing the easing of tension involved in listening to an utterly professional artist, which means just accepting the music without having to worry about difficult passages. With everyone else, we applauded pieces by Stravinsky and Prokofieff spontaneously and warmly and when the programme came to an end, we stamped our feet in unison to be allowed to hear some more.

Then Isaac played a simple little *Adagio* from a concerto by Haydn. Suddenly the concert was transformed into divine worship; I don't know how else to describe it. Time stood still and you felt it a favour to be allowed to be alive and experience such supernatural beauty. The notes from the instrument were so lovely, so warm and natural, they struck your nervous system like rays from the sun. The relatively simply constructed music, really only a C-minor scale, became a ladder straight up to eternity. When Stern had finished, for a few moments there was absolute total silence, and then the enthusiastic cheering started again. I looked at Kjerstin and she looked at me, our cheeks wet with tears.

'I didn't know music could be like that,' said Kjerstin. 'What happened?'

Well, one may well ask. Does everything have to be dissected, or can such a moment be retained for the rest of one's life without explanations?

# 14/ So Many Deaths

When the time comes for my last moment, I cannot complain that I have not had enough training. A large part of my life has been spent dying and studying how various dying people behave shortly before or during their last moment. I am convinced that just before I draw my last breath, recognising the situation, I will think: 'Ah, yes, this is what I did in *Bohème*, isn't it . . .' or whatever it is it reminds me of.

When my father stopped breathing after lying unconscious for a week, I had been sitting beside him for several days, hoping that he would regain consciousness. We never looked in each other's eyes again, but through our hands, it felt to me as if he knew I was with him. When they told me he was dead, it struck me: 'He has done just what I usually do in Mélisande's death-scene. Every breath, every small movement of the head and hands was the same.'

When I next played Mélisande, of course, I lived through my father's death all over again and ruined the scene by letting the audience see a weeping corpse.

My mother chose to die like Traviata. She sat up in her sick-bed with a surprised and exalted expression on her face and then fell straight back. That is just what I do when Violetta has sung her last note.

Putting myself inside what is happening in a person before the thread of life is snapped is probably what has meant most to me in life. Perhaps it has also occasionally been of some help in the depressions that inevitably occur at different stages of life. We who also live on the stage have the advantage of being allowed to live out a number of problems . . . but we pay the price by sometimes not knowing who we are. If over the years you have played a great number of different rôles, it is all too easy in your private life to hide yourself inside those people, borrowing a bit here and there.

This also works in another direction: you go round watching your fellow human beings, observing their characteristics, and then you use part of one and part of another when you create your characters.

When I was to play such parts as Alcestis or Iphigenia, I found it very difficult. These Greek heroines are ordained by the gods to sacrifice their lives, Alcestis so that her sick husband shall regain his health and the country their king. Iphigenia's life is sacrificed for what in my view is a silly reason, so that King Menelaus shall have favourable winds when his fleet is to sail for Troy to bring back the faithless Helen.

Firstly, my common sense told me that all that about the will of the gods was sheer bluff, simply intriguing people concocting it all for political reasons and persuading the people that the idea of human sacrifice came from higher powers. Secondly, I considered Queen Alcestis had just as much right to go on living for her children as their father the King had. But the more I became involved in the fates of these women, the more I understood how much it meant to them suddenly to have a great purpose in their lives. To be able to show by such an action how strong the wife's love, and then the daughter's, was for her husband, or father,

94

gave the woman a strength which immediately made her equal to the man. So through these rôles I found some perspective on man's situation throughout the centuries. By tradition it has always been considered quite natural that every man should be prepared to sacrifice his life at any time, for his country, or for peace, or for whatever reason is thought up to encourage male individuals to march off to their deaths or to put others to death.

So many deaths . . . I have been strangled, I have been stabbed, I have died of consumption, heartbreak and plague, and I have taken my own life by hara-kiri, taking pills, by drowning myself.

Among the most interesting deaths I have experienced was when Emilia Marty hands over the paper on which is the formula that would give her three hundred more years of life.

In the opera by Janacek called *The Makropoulos Case*, I played this woman who is three hundred years old. As a girl in 1585, she was forced to swallow a drink that Emperor Ferdinand had ordered from his court physician, the drink that would give him three hundred years to live. Her reaction to this makes the Emperor believe that the drink is poisoned. The physician is executed, and when the girl gradually regains consciousness, she has to flee the country. But the formula has worked, Emilia lived on and on to discover all the problems such a life entailed. She was constantly forced to flee to new stopping-places, and could not reveal herself by staying any length of time in each place.

When the opera starts, she is desperate. The paper with the formula on it has been lost. She has initiated one of her lovers into her secret, lent him the formula and then parted from him. Now she sees in the newspapers that there is a dispute over his will, and she hopes to find her paper among his possessions. There is some hurry, as she is, after all, three-hundred-and-thirty-seven and in need of another dose. The intrigue is complicated, but the whole opera demonstrates that eternal life does not bring happiness, and that everything is simply repeated. Emilia has become cynical, bitter and blasé. When she finally stands with the magic paper in her hand, she has been forced to tell the whole story, and with that has herself realised that eternal life is not worth striving for. She is tired and wishes to come to rest. She offers the paper to a young girl, but the girl is frightened of becoming like Emilia and burns it . . . at that moment, Emilia sinks to the ground.

When I was working on this rôle, I was surrounded by people who kept saying they would very much like to live a little longer to be there for this, or that, or the other. And suddenly I saw us all from the outside . . . I realised how meaningless it was to strive thus. Positions are simply changed all the time. At this stage in my life, I have long since realised that I will never have time to tackle all the music I long to, I'll never have time to read all the books I want to, I'll never be able to go to all the places I want to see. So, I take one day at a time and try to live life while I'm alive and let fate decide when it has to come to an end.

The most difficult thing in a performance in which you have died is to get up again and go and take a curtain-call. It seems so false and wrong that I feel physically ill. But when I once complained about this to someone who had been in the auditorium, this was the reply : 'Thank heavens we were able to see you again. Otherwise it would have been impossible to go home.'

Once I was very near death in my real life. I lay bleeding to death in bed. There was no help available at the time, and I could feel myself getting weaker and weaker. I was convinced I was about to die. During the last minutes before I was saved, I had but one thought in my head which ground on and on and on: 'Oh, how marvellous, now I never need be reviewed by that malicious critic Nyblom again.'

# 15/ The Long and the Short of It

The night of the première of my first rôle at the Royal Opera, I thought I would stand myself a taxi down to the opera.

'Please take me to the Royal Theatre in Gustaf Adolf Square,' I said to the driver.

He turned round and looked at me.

'Are you an opera-singer?'

'Yes,' I said proudly.

He drove on in silence for a while, then said, 'You're young and not bad-looking. Wouldn't it be a good idea if you changed profession while there's still time?'

In 1947, opera was considered a dying art. Even during the 1950s, it was highly suspect to devote yourself to opera. I have stood at the barricades for the major part of my career, defending the art form to which I have devoted my life.

So it is good to look back on developments since and see that opera is still alive and despite all the practical difficulties, now flourishes more than ever before. Records, radio and television have all helped to make operatic music available to more and more people, and an acquaintance with classical or serious music has delighted, helped or entertained many people who before would never have dreamt of benefiting from what is often scornfully labelled 'culture'.

'Fancy having such a gift,' people often say to us. 'Fancy

98

being able to please so many people with your singing.'

At first I thought that silly. I was on the stage for my own sake. If there were anyone I wanted to please, it was myself, and I swore a secret oath that the moment I ceased to enjoy it, I would give it up.

Over the years, however, I have discovered that the most wonderful thing about this profession is to be able to share the joy I feel in music-making. Trying to transmit beauty, drama and romance in words and notes, thus knowing that a number of people have been involved in the atmosphere you have managed to create . . . that means you gladly put up with a life that cannot be called either comfortable or healthy by today's standards of values.

If an artist paints a picture, he can exhibit it and people can come to look at it. If they don't immediately understand all the details of it, they can look at it a second or even a third time. They can look at it from the right and from the left, seeing it in different lights.

If a writer writes a novel or a poem or a play, people can read it when it suits them, and if they don't understand what it says the first time, they can read it again and think about it.

When a composer creates a work of music, in order that it shall reach other people, it has to be put into the hands of an interpreter, and before it can be experienced, it thus has to be filtered through someone else's personality.

I often feel that mediating music is an enormously responsible assignment, especially contemporary music. If you have the opportunity to work together with the composer, you may get some guidance. He can to some extent explain how he had thought it should sound. But all the same, you perhaps cannot get it to sound as it had done inside his head, and very often rehearsal-time is far too short to achieve an ideal interpretation. There is perhaps only *one* performance, and in that time, the audience has to try to acquire some understanding of the details of the work, which it has often taken the mediator months of work to grasp. Whether listeners like the music or not depends to a great extent on the performance it gets. If I am not feeling inspired, am not on good form, or am not sufficiently prepared, then I can kill a piece of music before it has a chance to live. But it can happen that you help to launch a work, to arouse the interest of the audience and other artists, so that it is taken up elsewhere, and when that happens, it is immensely pleasing.

One of the things that has most fascinated me over the years that I have spent performing in public is where the borderline between the sublime and the ridiculous lies? Why is it so easy to overstep the mark when you are so eager to do your very best, and then just overdo it? A voice that does not carry properly in that great cry that is supposed to express despair or anguish . . . and the audience laughs.

Why is opera so often regarded as something foolish? Is it because we try to emphasise with strong expressions what the music has already said? All my life I have striven to show that it is not in the slightest unnatural to express yourself in song, and one of the things that has made me most happy is when people have sometimes written about my performances that 'the drama was so gripping that you didn't think about her singing'. Then I have perhaps been able to find a balance between music, words and gestures, and have achieved the work of art I consider an opera performance should be.

Often, very often, all too often some people say, I have played with fire. I have mixed serious numbers with parody. It is like a challenge. I enjoy it immensely when at one moment I can tempt the audience into laughter and the next moment bewitch them with the seriousness of the music I am singing. I have quite consciously worked in this way when I have given concerts of music considered 'difficult'. First I talk about the music I am to perform, and try to make that entertaining. I try as lightly as possible to describe tragic atmospheres, too, or events the music is about. In this way, I myself can also relax and the audience is more open and receptive to suggestion.

This all started during my adolescence and opera-school years, when I gave concerts to audiences who were not familiar with and did not really want to hear the kind of music I was performing. I stubbornly refused to 'lower' my musical standards. I was going to evangelise. I *would* make them like classical music. And it often went well, once you could tear down the walls of prejudice and misunderstanding and not get on your high horse. Presuming that everyone in a concert audience understands foreign languages is simply wrong. Thinking that everyone has bought or read the texts in the programme is a mistake. Better to take the risk that those who do know and understand are exposed to what they sometimes consider an insult. 'Does she think we're so uneducated?' I stand on the platform to sing *to* and not *for* an audience.

This has nothing to do with snobbery or attempts to educate people. It is an intense desire to be allowed to share the worlds of beauty from which I myself derive such endless stimulation.

I once took part in one of those affairs in which an artist is expected to practise his or her profession with enthusiasm for no payment, a charity concert arranged by one of the Stockholm daily papers. Among those taking part, the name of Snoddas, a very well-known singer of popular songs, was in letters ten centimetres high, and my name was a long way down the list of participants.

My performance was not very successful. Most of the people in the audience had certainly come to the Concert Hall to hear Snoddas and were not familiar with romantic songs, so they applauded immediately after the first verse of Grieg's *Spring*. Nevertheless, I sang another verse, and when I had finished, the audience was deathly silent, so in dismay, I stammered: 'That's the end', at which I received some scattered applause that died away before I had even reached the wings. Needless to say, I wept bitterly in amongst the overcoats.

I happened to be in the crowd pouring out of the hall when it was all over and I heard two ladies talking.

'He's wonderful, isn't he, Snoddas!'

'Yes, but I thought Elisabeth Söderström sang well, too.'

'Her, yes . . . but she's studied and learnt it all.'

Culture's problem in a nutshell.